The Magic of Words

The Magic of Words

A Supplement to **Childcraft—The How and Why Library**

Field Enterprises Educational Corporation
Chicago   Frankfurt   London   Paris   Rome   Sydney   Tokyo   Toronto

Acknowledgments

The publishers of *Childcraft—The How and Why Library*
gratefully acknowledge the courtesy of the following
publisher for permission to use copyrighted material in
this volume. Full illustration acknowledgments appear
on page 298.

Page 130: "Waltzing Matilda," copyright 1936 by Allan
& Co., Prop. Ltd. Melbourne, Australia. International
copyright secured. Copyright renewed. Used by permission
of Carl Fischer, Inc., New York.

Preface

You can make magic!

Say the word *dog*. That word is just a noise that you make with your tongue and throat. But anyone who hears it will think of a four-footed animal that barks and wags its tail. So, with nothing but a noise, you can put a picture of a dog in other peoples' minds. And that's a sort of magic—the magic of words!

Words and language are marvelous things. With words people can let each other know what they're thinking. They can put pictures into each others' minds. With words, people can share ideas, and knowledge, and fun. No other creature on earth can do such things. Only humans have the magic of words.

Did you ever wonder where these noises we call words came from—how they began? Most of them have stories to tell. Many of the words you use come from long ago. They've been through many adventures. You use words that sailed with the hardy Vikings and rode with the armored knights of Normandy. You use words that were made up by Greek explorers in Egypt thousands of years ago. There's a tale behind most words—a tale that may be surprising, amusing, or exciting.

Come now, and find out about these wonderful things called words. Find out what some of the words you use really mean—why you call a certain kind of dog a *poodle*, and why the top of a house is called a *roof*. Find out what names mean, for names are words, too. Discover the marvelous adventure story of your language, and the fascinating tale of how writing came to be. Find out the many ways you can use words for fun and entertainment. You're in for a real treat, learning about *The Magic of Words!*

The Magic of Words

Contents

9   **There's a Hippo in the Attic, Eating a Sandwich**
Stories of the origins of many everyday words

47   **Names Are Words, Too**
The meanings of many first and last names

67   **The Tale of the English Tongue**
The exciting, true story of how the English language came to be, and how it has grown and changed during some fifteen hundred years

127   **English Everywhere**
Different ways of speaking English in different parts of the world

141   **From Sounds to Letters**
The story of the invention of writing and the alphabet

213   **People Who Work with Words**
The work of writers, reporters, newscasters, teachers, and others who make a living using words

231   **Fun with Words**
Rebuses, riddles, puns, tongue twisters, crossword puzzles, codes, ciphers, and other activities that depend on word skill

290   **Books to Read**

294   **New Words**

298   **Illustration Acknowledgments**

299   **Index**

There's a

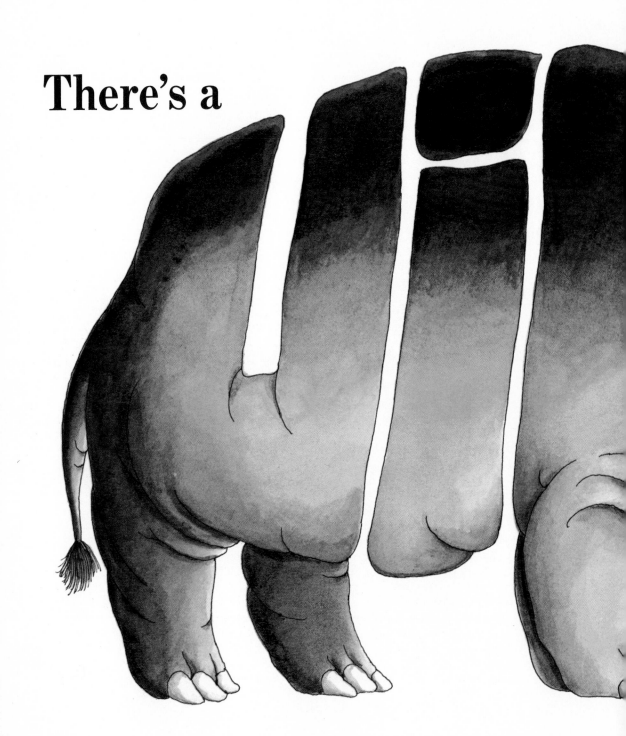

in the Attic, Eating a Sandwich

Most words are names of things—creatures, objects, or actions. But why do we call things by certain names? You know that a hippopotamus is a certain kind of animal—but *why* is it called a hippopotamus? You know what an attic is, and what a sandwich is. But how did they get these names? There's a wonderful story behind most words—and here are some of the stories.

Menu
Clam Chowder
Hamburger
Sandwich
coleslaw
French Fries
Chocolate Sundae

Menu meanings

That looks like a pretty good lunch, doesn't it! But where did these rather strange names come from? Why do we call a lump of ground beef a *ham*burger? What in the world does *coleslaw* mean? And why is a dish of ice cream with chocolate syrup called a *sundae*?

Here's how each of the foods on this menu got its name.

Clam chowder is a soup made out of clams and vegetables. Soup is usually cooked in a big pot. And our word *chowder* comes from the French word *chaudiere*, which means "pot."

There is no ham at all in hamburger. It's made of ground beef. Americans think of hamburger as being an American food, but it really came from Germany. Long ago, many German people came to America to live. They brought with them a lot of recipes for their favorite foods. One of these foods was a kind of meat ball made of ground beef. These meat balls were supposed to have been invented in the German city of Hamburg, so they became known as hamburgers.

But why should a hamburger between two pieces of bread be called a *sandwich*?

The word *sandwich* comes from the name of an English

Menu meanings

(continued from page 11)

town. Long ago, the town of Sandwich was owned by a nobleman, called the Earl of Sandwich. The earl loved to play cards. One day, he was playing cards and didn't want to stop for dinner, even though he was hungry. So he told a servant to bring him some slices of meat between two pieces of toasted bread. Others tried this new way of eating bread and meat together. They called it a *sandwich* in honor of the earl. To this day, any kind of food that is served between slices of bread is called a sandwich.

Coleslaw is a spicy salad made of chopped cabbage, and that's exactly what its name means. This salad came from Holland. Its name is made up of two Dutch words—*kool*, meaning "cabbage,"

sandwich

and *sla,* meaning "salad." So *coleslaw* simply means "cabbage salad."

You might think that French fried potatoes got their name because they were first made in France. But that's not the reason. Cooks at hotels and restaurants often cut meat and vegetables into long strips. This is called *Frenching.* So when potatoes are cut into strips they are Frenched. Frenched potatoes that were fried were first called Frenched fried potatoes, but now we just call them French fries.

Do you like catchup, or ketchup, on your French fries? Lots of people do. It gives the French fries a tangy taste. Catchup and ketchup are two different names for a tomato sauce. They both come from the Chinese word *ke-tsiap,* which means "taste." So, when you put

french fries

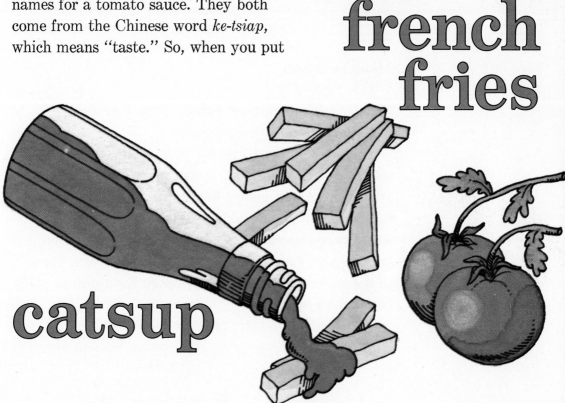

catsup

Sundae

Menu meanings
(continued from page 13)

tomato catchup on your French fries, you're simply putting tomato taste on them.

There are many stories about how the ice cream sundae got its name. One story comes from Manitowoc, Wisconsin. About eighty-five years ago, sundaes were rather special. You could get them only in little stores called ice cream parlors, and you could usually get them only on a Sunday. They had no name then, so if you wanted one, you just asked for a dish of "special ice cream."

One weekday, a little girl came into Mr. George Giffy's ice cream parlor in Manitowoc. She asked for

A dish of the special ice cream, please.

a dish of the special ice cream. Mr. Giffy told her that he sold the special ice cream only on Sunday.

"Then this must be Sunday," said the little girl, "because that's the kind of ice cream I want." That gave Mr. Giffy the idea to begin calling the special ice cream a "Sunday." And, somehow, it later got turned into "sundae."

According to another story, the sundae got its name in Evanston, Illinois. A dish of ice cream with syrup was called a "Sunday soda" there. But some people didn't like having a dish of ice cream named after Sunday—the Sabbath—so "Sunday soda" got changed to "sundae soda" and then just "sundae."

However it got its name, a sundae is still a treat!

hippopotamus

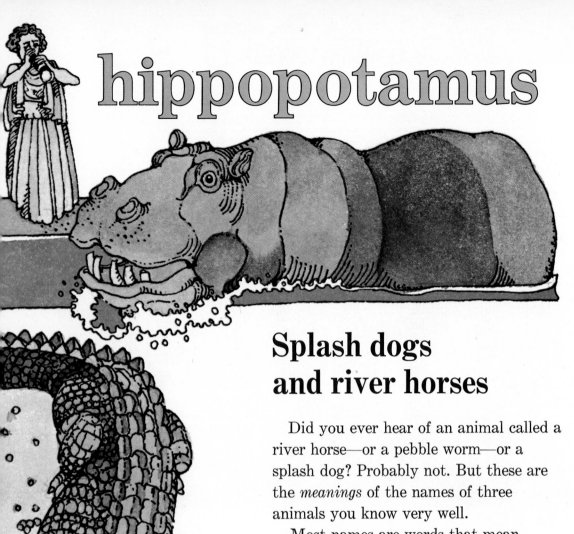

Splash dogs
and river horses

Did you ever hear of an animal called a river horse—or a pebble worm—or a splash dog? Probably not. But these are the *meanings* of the names of three animals you know very well.

Most names are words that mean something. Sometimes, the things they mean are funny or surprising.

The hippopotamus was named by the ancient Greeks. The first Greeks who saw a hippopotamus snorting and splashing in a river must have thought it looked like a fat horse, because the word *hippopotamus* means "river horse" in Greek.

The ancient Greeks also gave the

crocodile
poodle

spider

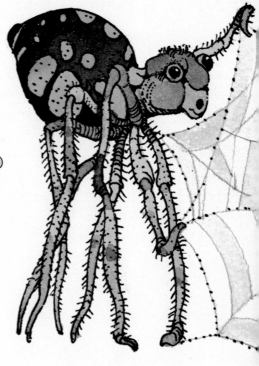

crocodile its name. The first crocodile they saw must have been lying with its feet tucked under it on a gravel beach, so that it looked like a legless worm. The Greeks put together their words for *pebble* and *worm* to make the word *krokodilos*, which means "pebble worm."

Poodle comes from the German word *Pudelhund*. In German, *pudeln* means "to splash water," and *hund* means "dog." So a poodle is a "splash dog."

Our name for the bug called a beetle comes from the Old English word *bitula*, which means "biter."

Spider also comes from an Old English word, *spithre*, which means "spinner."

Duck is from the Old English word *duce*. Pronounced *dook uh*, it means "diver." This is a good name, because

duck

Megalo

Splash dogs and river horses
(continued from page 17)

ducks dive down in the water to get their food.

The names of many North American animals come from Indian words. The word *moose* is almost like the Algonkian word *moos-u,* which means "he strips off bark." The Indians gave this big animal that name because when he's very hungry he eats bark that he strips off young trees.

The name *octopus* comes from two Greek words— *okto,* meaning "eight," and *pous,* meaning "foot." So

saurus

octopus means "eight-footed," because this animal has eight wiggly tentacles.

One of the last kinds of animals to be named were the dinosaurs. When dinosaur bones were first discovered, scientists used Greek and Latin words to make up names that would best describe these great reptiles. The first dinosaur to be named was Megalosaurus. Scientists thought it was a giant lizard. They named it by combining two Greek words, *megalou,* meaning "great," and *sauros,* meaning "lizard." So *Megalosaurus* simply means "great lizard."

Wind-eyes in the posts

It's spring-cleaning time at your house. You're going to wash the wind-eyes in the elegant room. Then you're going to help your mother paint the posts in the cooking place.

That sounds strange, doesn't it? But, as a matter of fact, every house really does have lots of "wind-eyes," "posts" in every room, a "cooking place," and, usually, an "elegant room," too. It also has "pieces of windows," and "splits" on its "cover"!

What are wind-eyes? Well, long ago, Vikings living in Britain had openings in the walls of their houses to let in light and air. To the Vikings, the openings seemed like eyes looking out at the wind. So they called them "wind-eyes." Their word for "wind-eye" was *vindauga*—and that's where our word *window* comes from. So *window* really means "wind-eye."

And what about the glass in a window—the panes? How did they get this name? At one time, people used pieces of cloth to cover the window openings in walls. Long ago, in England, such a piece of cloth was called a *pannus*, meaning "a piece of cloth." Later, that word was changed to *pan*, and then *pane*, and simply meant

Coquina!

Wind-eyes in the posts

(continued from page 21)

"piece." Thus, a windowpane is a window "piece."

We could call the attic of a house the "elegant room." This seems a strange name for a room that's usually full of junk. But here's how it works out.

Many people in England once thought the ancient Greek city of Athens must have been the most elegant and beautiful place in the world. They changed the Greek word *Attikos*, which means "of Athens" to *Attic*, and used it to mean something that was truly elegant. They built houses with rows of pillars along the top, as the Greeks had done. These pillars were said to be "Attic style." After a while, people called the whole top part of such a house an *attic*. So, the word *attic*, our name for the dusty, junk-filled room at the top of a house, really means something fine and elegant, like ancient Athens.

The part of a house where cooking is done is the kitchen. Why not just call this room the "cooking room"? How did it get the odd name *kitchen*?

The word *kitchen* comes from the Latin word *coquina*,

Cooking place!

which means "cooking." Roman soldiers took that word into Britain, where it became *cychene*, and meant a place where cooking was done. *Cychene* became *kuchene*, and finally *kitchen*. So kitchen really means "a cooking place."

The "posts" in every room in a house are the walls. Long ago, when a Roman army made camp, the soldiers put walls around the camp's four sides. The walls were made of wooden posts pounded into the ground. The Roman word for *post* was *vallus*, and the wall of posts was called a *vallum*. So, our word *wall*, which comes from *vallum*, means "a row of posts."

And, last of all, every house has a cover with splits on it. Our word *roof* comes from the Old English word *hrof*, meaning "cover." Roofs have shingles, and shingles used to be made of pieces of wood that had been split. The Latin word *scindula* means "split." In English, this word was changed to *shindle* and then to *shingle*. So a house with a shingle roof has a "cover" with "splits."

And that's the story of the wind-eyes, elegant room, posts, cover, and splits of your house.

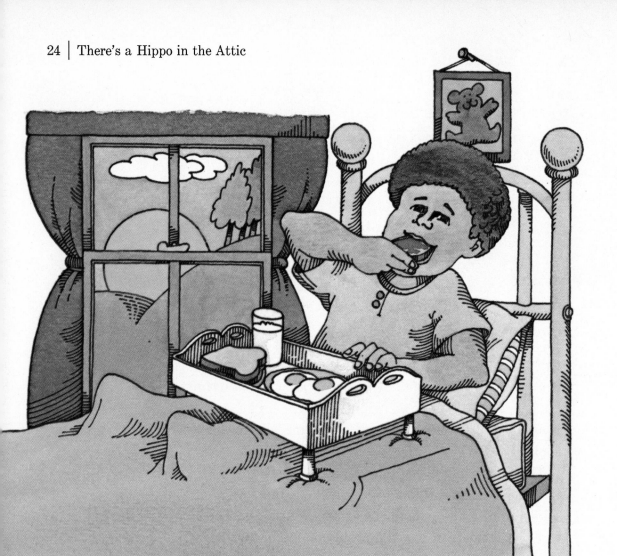

A break, a lump, and a sip

Have you ever broken a fast?

Yes, you have, lots of times. And you were never blamed for breaking it!

Fast doesn't only mean "quick," it also means to go without eating. You fast all night long, while you're asleep. Then, when you wake up in the morning and eat, you *break* your fast—that is, you stop fasting. And that's why we call our morning meal breakfast.

At noontime you eat a lump! The word *lunch* first

JEAN-N-N, COME SiP.

meant a lump of bread. There was also an old word, *nuncheon*, which meant a noontime drink. Word experts think this was changed to *luncheon*, meaning a lump of food at noontime.

Evening is suppertime. Supper is usually your biggest meal, so you'd be surprised if your mother gave you only soup and told you to "sip it." But that's what *supper* really means. It comes from the older word *sup*, which meant to sip a liquid. Nowadays, people usually say, "Let's have supper." Long ago, they were more likely to say, "Let us sup."

Wear words

Pants is a funny-sounding word. Where did such a word come from?

A long time ago, many plays had a character called Pantalone. And Pantalone usually wore long, red tights. The first kind of long trousers that men wore were quite tight-fitting, so they became known as *pantaloons*, after Pantalone's long tights. But because *pantaloons* is such a long word, it was soon shortened to *pants*. And that's what it has been, ever since.

Lots of people wear pants called *jeans*, *denims*, *dungarees*, or *Levi's*. These are all pants made out of strong cotton cloth, usually dyed blue. How did they get all these strange names?

Jeans comes from the name *Genes*, which is the

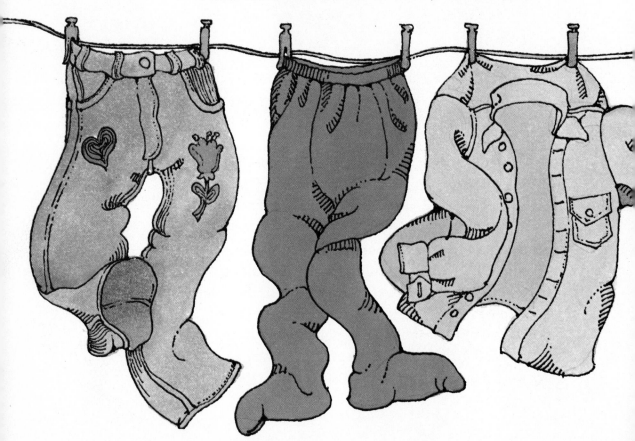

French name for the city of Genoa, Italy, where a lot of cotton cloth was made. French people called the cloth by their name for the city. We use the French name as our word for the pants.

Another kind of strong cotton cloth was made in the city of Nimes, France. The cloth was called *serge de Nimes*. And, of course, *denims* comes from *de Nimes*.

Dungarees comes from the East Indian word *dungri*. Long ago, English traders brought coarse cotton cloth called *dungri* back from India. In time, the English people changed the word to dungaree.

Levi's are named after a man, Levi Strauss. He was a clothing merchant who put metal fasteners on the pockets of pants to keep them from tearing.

Perhaps you've wondered about the word *clothes*. *Clothes* simply means "cloths"—the cloths you wear.

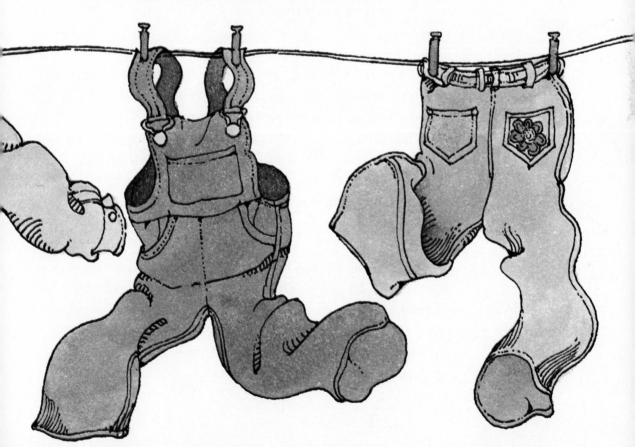

School

School words

Believe it or not, *school* means "spare time!"

The ancient Greeks believed that education was one
of the most important things in life. Young Greeks
would even use their spare time for learning. They
liked to listen to wise men talk about science and other
things. The Greek word *schole*, means "spare time." A
group of young Greeks who listened to teachers in
their spare time was called a *schole*. And, of course,
that's where our word *school* comes from.

Your schoolbooks owe their name to a tree. People
in England once wrote on the thin, inner bark of
beech trees. In Old English, the name of the beech tree
was *boc*. After a while, *boc*, then *bok*, and finally *book*
came to mean the writing on a sheet of bark. Now
it means many sheets of paper, with writing or printing
on them, all bound together.

The pen that you do your schoolwork with is named
after a feather. For hundreds of years people wrote
with feathers. They cut the quills to a point and
dipped them in ink. The Latin word for feather is
penna, and so the feathers used for writing became
known as *pens*. And to this day, we still call any
writing tool that uses ink a *pen*.

The word *pencil* comes from a Latin word, too. The
word is *penicillus*, and means "brush" or "little tail."
Artists used to call their smallest, pointed brushes
pencils, because the brush looked like a little pointed
tail. In time, the name came to be used for the
pointed writing tool we call a pencil.

And why are you and your schoolmates called pupils?
The Latin word *pupillae* means "little dolls." Long
ago, that word came to mean children who were in the
care of a teacher. It is from this word that we got
the English word, *pupil*.

Bearders and tellers

It's easy to understand what the names of some jobs mean. A *lawyer* works with the law. A *teacher* teaches.

But many job names don't seem to have anything to do with the job itself. Why is a person who gives haircuts called a barber? And why is a person who works in a store called a clerk?

Barbers not only give haircuts, they also shave men. And that's how they got their name. The Latin word for beard was *barba*, so a man who shaves and trims beards is a barber, meaning "a bearder."

Long ago, in Europe, a priest or monk was called a cleric. That's a Latin word that means "priest." Priests, or clerics, were once just about the only people who knew how to read, write, and do arithmetic. So, they kept all the written records for kings and nobles. They figured

out how much people owed in taxes, kept records of payments, and so on.

Hundreds of years later, when many people other than priests could read and write, anyone who kept written records, or worked with figures, was called a cleric. Later, this was shortened to clerk. People who work in stores and offices do a lot of writing and figuring, so they became known as clerks. If you know people who are clerks, they'll be surprised when you tell them that the name of their job really means "priest."

You might think that someone who is called a teller would tell things to people. But tellers work in banks. They count out money. The word *teller* really means "counter."

Why do we call the people who deliver letters and packages *mail* carriers when they're really carrying letters? It's because, hundreds of years ago, in France,

Bearders and tellers
(continued from page 31)

the first letter carriers had leather bags called *males* to carry letters in. When the people of England started having men deliver letters, the name of the bag was borrowed from the French. But the spelling became *mail* instead of *male*. So *mail* really means "a leather bag," and a mail carrier is a "bag carrier."

Today, an engineer is a person who plans and builds roads, dams, bridges, buildings, airplanes, ships, and many other things. But long ago, an engineer was part of an army. In those days, armies often had to capture cities and castles. But the cities and castles had high walls, so the armies had to try to knock down the walls or get over them. To do this, they used machines. They had tall wooden towers to get men over the walls, battering rams to pound the walls until they fell down, and catapults that hurled huge rocks at the walls. These machines were called war engines. The word *engine* meant both "skill" and "invention." The men who built the machines were called engineers, meaning "skilled inventors." And that's what we still call people who plan and build things.

A person who owns or works in a grocery store is called a grocer. The word *grocer* comes from the word *gross*, which means "a large amount." Hundreds of years ago, there were no food stores, just stores where you could buy spices. The men who owned such stores were called *spicers en gross*, which meant "spice sellers in large amounts." But people shortened this to *grosser*, and spelled it *grocer*. So when people started to sell large amounts of all kinds of food, they were called grocers, and their stores became known as grocery stores.

Lazy words

When it comes to words, most people are a little lazy. They don't like to take the time to say words that seem too long. So they shorten the words by using only part of them. Our language is full of such parts-of-words.

Bus is a part-of-a-word. It comes from the word *omnibus*. People who lived in cities once had to walk to get from one place to another. Only wealthy people

who owned horses or carriages, were able to get about quickly and easily. But about 150 years ago, in France, big carriages were used to make it easier for everyone to get about in the city of Paris. These carriages traveled back and forth on many of the city's streets, picking up people who wanted to go somewhere. It cost very little to ride on one of these carriages, so almost everyone could afford it.

Because the carriages were for everyone, they were given the name omnibus, which is a Latin word that

Lazy words
(continued from page 35)

means "for all." Soon, omnibuses were put to work in English cities, too. But there, the people quickly shortened the name to bus.

Gun is really part of the word *dragon*. The first guns were sometimes called dragons because they shot out smoke and fire, the way dragons are supposed to.

Cab is short for the French word *cabriolet*, which comes from a word meaning "to leap or caper." And a

cabriolet was a light, two-wheeled carriage that bounced a lot, so the name was a good one.

Are you a baseball or football fan? This kind of fan comes from the word *fanatic*. A fanatic is someone who gets wildly excited about something he or she believes in.

Mathematics, photograph, advertisement, telephone, airplane, and *examination* are all words that we often shorten—such as saying *ad* for *advertisement*. What lazy words have been made from the others?

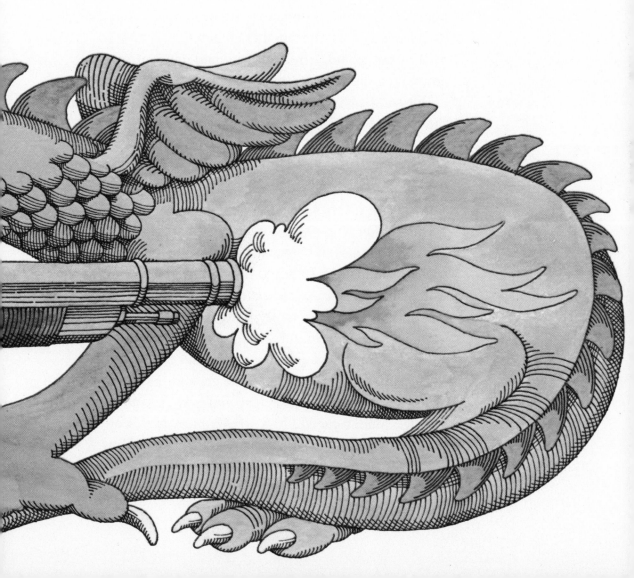

Howls, thumps, and creaks

It was midnight, and the sky was black and stormy! The wind *howled*, and there were *crashes* of thunder. Rain *pattered* sharply on the roof of the old haunted house. A shutter, swinging in the wind, went *bang-bang, bang-bang* against the side of the house.

"I'm not afraid," the boy who had gone into the house on a dare said to himself.

But suddenly, he heard another noise. From down in the cellar there came the long, slow *creak* of a door opening. The boy's hair stood up with fright as he heard the *clank* of dragging chains. Then—*thump* . . . *thump* . . . *thump*. Something was coming up the stairs! With a *shriek*, the boy rushed out of the house.

One reason why ghost stories are so much fun is because they use words that help us imagine the spooky sounds of a haunted house at night. For words such as *howl, crash, patter, bang, creak, clank, thump*, and *shriek* are really imitations of sounds.

Our language is full of words that imitate sounds. *Thud* is a word that imitates the sound something heavy makes when it falls to the ground. *Squish* sounds like the noise your feet make when you walk through mud. *Squawk, bark, croak, purr, buzz*, and *grunt* sound like noises certain animals make. How many other noise-words can you think of?

Nice villains
and naughty chairs

Can a villain be nice? Can a chair be naughty?

Once, long ago, they could. Many of the words we use once had different meanings. *Nice*, *villain*, and *naughty* all meant something quite different from what they do now.

Nice once meant "stupid." It comes from the Latin word *nescius*, which means "not knowing." A nice person was once someone who didn't know anything!

Today, a villain is a bad person. But the word *villain* once simply meant "a farmer." In Latin, a *villa* was a big farmhouse, owned by a rich man or noble. A *vilanus* was a man who worked the farmlands that belonged to the *villa*. The word *vilanus* got changed to *villein* in French, and then to *villain* in

English. Because the villains had poor manners and no education, the nobles looked down on them, as if they were bad people. So, slowly, the word *villain* came to mean someone who was wicked.

Long ago, someone might have said that a chair was naughty. A naughty chair would have been a chair that wasn't much good. *Naughty* meant "good for nothing." It comes from the word *naught*, which we still use to mean "nothing."

Quick used to mean "alive" instead of "fast," as it does now. It comes from the Old English word *cwic*. When people said someone was quick, they meant that he was alive. When they wanted someone to do something in a hurry, they said, "be quick," meaning "be alive, move fast, like a live person." After a while, *quick* came to mean "fast," as it does now.

And if someone calls you "silly," you shouldn't care. *Silly* used to mean "happy."

Invented words

Suppose you invented a wonderful new kind of popcorn popper—one that didn't need electricity or fire, but simply popped corn when you *told* it to! What would you call such a great invention?

You could call it a dictapopper! The Latin word *dictare* means "to say or speak" so *dictapopper* would mean "pops when you speak."

Lots of inventions are named this

way—by putting together two or three words to make a brand new word that tells what the invention does. That's how the telephone, the automobile, and television got their names.

We use a telephone to send the sound of our voice to someone who is far away. And *telephone* means "far sound." It's a word that is made up from two Greek words—*tele*, which means "far," and *phone*, which means "sound."

If *telephone* means "far sound," can

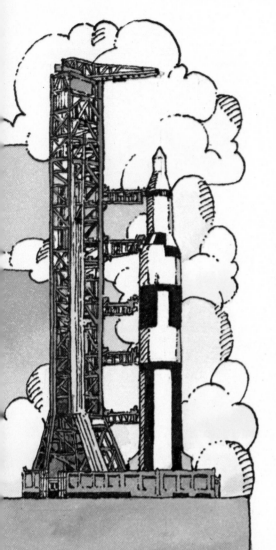

Invented words
(continued from page 43)

you guess what *television* means? That's right—it means "far sight."

For thousands of years, people rode in wagons, carts, and buggies that were pulled by horses. But an automobile doesn't need an animal to pull it. It moves by itself. So the word *automobile* was made up from the Greek word *autos*, meaning "self," and the French word *mobile*, meaning "moving."

A photograph is a picture that's made by letting light touch a piece of film. *Photograph* is made up from the Greek words *photos*, meaning "light," and *graphein*, which means "to draw, or write." Thus, *photograph* means "to draw with light."

Space travel is one of the very newest inventions. So when men first began to travel in space, a name had to be invented to describe what they did. The name is *astronaut*. It comes from two Greek words—*astro*, meaning "star," and *nautes*, meaning "sailor." An astronaut is a "star sailor"—someone who sails among the stars.

When new inventions are invented, new names have to be invented for the inventions!

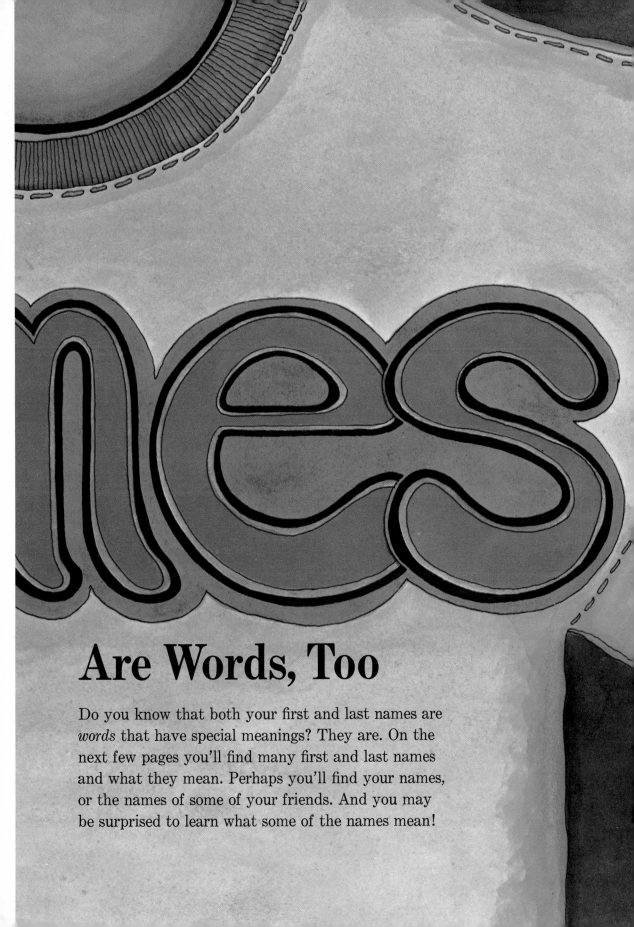

Are Words, Too

Do you know that both your first and last names are *words* that have special meanings? They are. On the next few pages you'll find many first and last names and what they mean. Perhaps you'll find your names, or the names of some of your friends. And you may be surprised to learn what some of the names mean!

What does your first name mean?

Are you a bee? That's what you are if your name is Deborah—for that's what Deborah means! Are you a wise advisor? You are if you're an Alfred! And even if you have no brothers or sisters, you're really a twin—if your name is Thomas!

Almost everyone's first name is a word that means something. Many of these word-names are thousands of years old. They come from many different languages.

Here are some names and what they mean. Perhaps you'll find the meaning of your name, or some of your friends' names. And you may be surprised!

Deborah

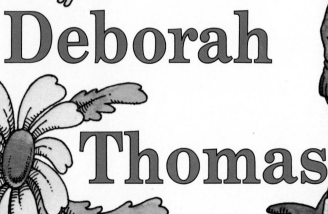

Thomas

Albert, Alberta, Bert, Bertha, Elaine, Eleanor, Ellen, Elena, Helen, Helene, Helena, and Lenore mean *bright*. Robert and Roberta mean *bright fame*.

Ellen

Enid, Catherine, Karen, Katherine, Kathleen, Kathryn, Kay, and Kitty mean *pure*.

Bess, Beth, Betsy, Betty, Elisa, Elsie, Elizabeth, and Lisa mean *belongs to God*.

Alice, Alicia, and Alison mean *truth*.

Russell

Rufus, Russell, and Rory mean *red-haired*.

Earl, Ethel, Patricia, Patrick, and Patsy mean *noble*.

Greta, Maggie, Mamie, Margaret, Margot, Marguerite, Marjorie, Meg, Peggy, and Rita mean *pearl*.

Greta

Debbie, Deborah, and Melissa mean *bee*.

Andrew, Carl, Carlo, Carol, Caroline, Carrie, Charles, Charlotte, and Karl mean *man* or *manly*.

Enrico, Hal, Harriet, Harry, Henry, and Henrietta, mean *master of a house*.

Enrico

Anthony, Antoinette, Antonia, Antonio, Antony, Toni, and Tony mean *great value*.

Esther, Ettie, Hester, and Stella mean *star*.

Brian

Brian and Ramsey mean *strong*.

Evan, Hans, Ian, Ivan, Jack, Jan, Jane, Janet, Janice, Jean, Jenny, Joan, Joanna, Johanna, John, Juan, Juanita, and Sean mean *God is gracious*.

Clarissa

Claire, Clara, Clarence, Clarice, Clarissa, and Rodney mean *famous*.

Barbara and Barbie mean *stranger*.

Basil, Eric, and Erica mean *royal*. Rex and Roy mean *king*. Riccardo and Richard mean *harsh king*.

Eric

Ann, Anna, Anne, Annette, Annie, and Hannah mean *grace*.

Sue, Susan, Susanna, Suzie, and Suzanne mean *graceful white lily*.

Errol and Wendy mean *wanderer*.

Wendy

Abigail, Abby, Gail, and Gayle mean *father's joy*.

Bartholomew, Bart, George, Georgette, and Georgina mean *farmer*.

George

Lewis, Lew, Louis, Louise, Luther, and Lulu mean *great warrior*.

Dee, Dora, Doreen, Dorothea, Dorothy, Ted, and Theodore mean *a gift of God*.

Mari, Maria, Marie, Marilyn, Marion, Marlene, Mary, Maureen, and Molly are thought to mean either *rebel* or *bitter*.

Alfreda

Alfred, Alfreda, and Conrad mean *wise advisor*.

Alastair, Alexander, Alexandra, Sandra, and Sandy mean *defender of man*.

How last names were invented

Once upon a time, four men lived on the same street in a little town. They all had the same name—Tom. And that was the only name any of them had. In those days, only kings and nobles had last names. Most men and women had only first names.

Because the men had the same name, you might think people would get them mixed up. But there was a way of telling them apart. One Tom had a father named John, so he was called *Tom, John's son*. Another Tom, a baker, was called *Tom the Baker*. The third Tom had light-colored hair. He was known as *Tom the White*. And the fourth Tom lived next to a park called the village green, so he was known to everyone as *Tom of the Green*.

Tom the Baker married a girl named Meg. She

became known as *Meg, Tom the Baker's wife*. They had a little boy named John, and he was known as *John, the Baker's son*. But after a while, people got tired of saying all those words. So they simply called Tom the Baker, *Tom Baker*. His wife became *Meg Baker*, and his son was *John Baker*.

That's how last names came to be. People took their father's first name, or the name of their job, or the name of the place where they lived, or a name that told how they looked. They put these names after their first names. When a man married, his wife and children took his last name. Sometimes, a widow or single woman might adopt children and give them her last name.

So, today, our last names can tell us something about the people we got them from, long ago—as you'll see in the next few pages.

Last names from first names

Before there were last names, children were often known by their father's name. If a man named Robert had a boy named John, the boy might be known as *John, Robert's*—meaning that he was Robert's son. If Robert had a daughter named Poll, she might be called *Poll, Robert's*. After a while, these became regular last names. When a boy grew up and married, he would give his last name to his wife and children. So, if your name ends with *s*, as in Roberts, Thomas, Adams, or Rogers, it came from someone who, long ago, had a father named Robert, Thomas, Adam, or Roger.

When people began to write last names, they often turned an *'s* ending of a name into *es*, *is*, or *ez*. Thus, names such as Jones and Hughes mean John's and

Wil

Jack, Wil's son

Hugh's. Names such as Davis, Harris, and Willis mean Davey's, Harry's, and Wil's. And Rodriguez and Hernandez mean Rodrigo's and Hernando's.

Boys were often called by their father's name with the word "son" added. If Wil had a son called Jack, the boy might be known as *Jack, Wil's son*. These kinds of names became regular last names, too. So if your last name ends in *son* or *sen*, as in Wilson, Johnson, Andersen, or Nelsen, you got it from someone whose father was named Wil, John, Anders, or Nels.

People who spoke other languages added "son" to their fathers' names, too. If your name ends in *sohn*, *wicz*, *vich*, or *ak*, those endings all mean "son."

People in some countries put their word for "son" in *front* of their fathers' names. *Mac*, *Mc*, and *Fitz* all mean "son of."

Jack, Wil's son, and the Wilson family

Iron pounders and clothes makers

Lots of last names come from the kind of work people did.

For hundreds of years, one of the most important jobs was making things out of metal, especially iron. Metalworkers made tools, weapons, horseshoes, lanterns, and other things people needed. To make these things, the metalworkers heated the iron until it was soft. Then they beat it into shape with hammers. In the Old English language, a person who shaped metal was called a *smith*. Metalworkers in other countries were also called by a word that in their language meant "to shape or forge metal."

There were lots of smiths. Nearly every community had one. When people began to take last names, most metalworkers

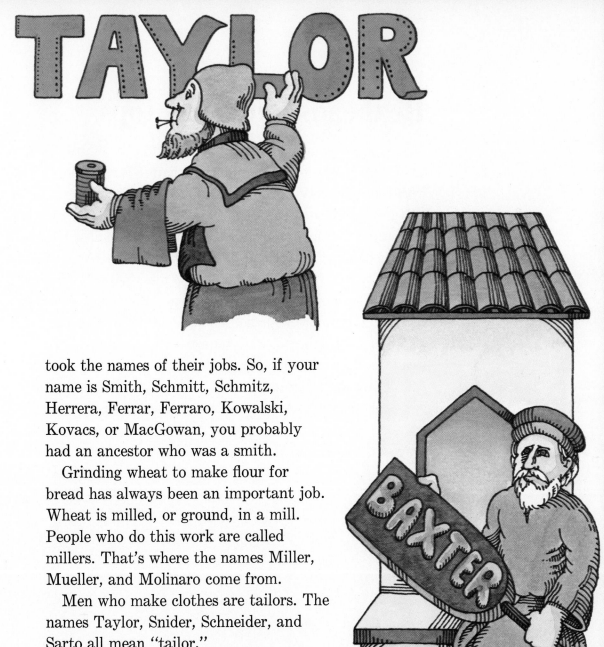

TAYLOR

took the names of their jobs. So, if your name is Smith, Schmitt, Schmitz, Herrera, Ferrar, Ferraro, Kowalski, Kovacs, or MacGowan, you probably had an ancestor who was a smith.

Grinding wheat to make flour for bread has always been an important job. Wheat is milled, or ground, in a mill. People who do this work are called millers. That's where the names Miller, Mueller, and Molinaro come from.

Men who make clothes are tailors. The names Taylor, Snider, Schneider, and Sarto all mean "tailor."

People once drove carts and wagons for a living, just as they drive trucks today. If your name is Carter, Porter, Wagner, or Schroeder, you probably got the name from someone who drove a cart or wagon.

Is your name Baker, Baxter, Fournier, Piekarz, or Boulanger? If so, you may have had an ancestor who was a baker.

Redheads and curly tops

Are any of your friends nicknamed "Red," "Whitey," or "Curly"? These are common nicknames for people with red hair, very light blond hair, and curly hair.

Hundreds of years ago, many people took such nicknames for their last names. A man might call himself "John White Head," or "Will the Red," or "Tom Curly." If your last name is White, Wise, Weiss, Whitehead, Whitlock, Whitman, Blanchard, Blount, or Bannon, your name may come from someone who had very light hair. If you are a Reed, Reid, Read, Roth, Russell, or Flynn, your name means "red." And if you are a Krause, Kruse, Cassidy, or Rizzo, you probably had an ancestor who was a "Curly."

Here cometh a
new man to town.

Many other nicknames also became last names. Names such as Long, Lang, Hoch, and Longfellow were nicknames for tall people. Little, Short, Small, Bass, Basset, Kline, Klein, Cline, Kurtz, Block, and Grubb were nicknames for people who were short. If your last name is Gay, Bliss, Murray, Froh, Merriman, Blaha, or Allegretti, you got your name from a good-natured person, for these names all mean "happy" or "cheerful."

In long-ago times, when last names were first used, most people seldom left the little towns where they were born. Everyone in a town knew everyone else. If a new person came to town to live, the people called him "new man," or "newcomer." After a while, he might take that for his last name. That's what Newman, Newcomb, Doyle, Doran, and Dowell mean.

Good morrow, Tom Long.

Did thee hear about Wil the White's wife?

Hills, brooks, and woods

Many last names come from places where people lived. A man named Robert, who lived on a hill, might call himself "Robert o' the Hill." A woman whose house was beside a brook might be known as "Nell of the Brook." After a while, these names were shortened to Robert Hill and Nell Brook.

Hill, Hull, Hillman, Downs, Downing, Lowe, Law, Knapp, Knowles, Peck, and Barrows are all names that come from people who lived on top of, on the side of, or at the bottom of a hill.

Brooks, Burns, Beck, Rivera, and Arroyo are names that come from people who lived beside a stream.

Wood, Woods, Atwood, Smallwood, Boyce, DuBois, Holt, Hurst, Shaw, and Silva are names that come from people who lived near small forests.

Marsh, Morse, Moore, Mosher, Carr, Carson, Kerr, Slaughter, and Tanaka are names that come from people who lived near a marsh, or swampy place.

Castle, Castillo, Castello, Zamecki, Burke, Burk, Borg, Burris, and Burr lived near a castle. Streeter, Lane, Strass, and Estrada lived near a road.

Lake, Lynn, Poole, and Pollard are all names that come from people who lived near lakes, ponds, or pools.

And Meadows, Mead, Field, Fields, Lee, Pratt, Vega, Murawski, and Campos are names that were given to people who lived near grassy fields.

Animals and birds

Some last names are the names of animals. This came about in one of several ways.

Hundreds of years ago, most signs had no writing on them—just a picture. Many of the signs in front of inns had a picture of an animal—a wolf, a bear, a lion, or some kind of bird. People who worked at inns, or lived near them, often took the name of the animal on the inn sign as their last name.

Other last names that are the names of animals come from nicknames. A man who was said to be "as smart as a fox" might have become known as Fox. And a very brave man might have been called Lion.

So, if your last name is the name of an animal, your name may have come from an ancestor who took the

name from a sign in front of an inn. Or, it may have been a nickname. Or, it may have been the name given to a man because he hunted a certain kind of animal.

The names Wolf, Wolfe, Wolff, and Lupo all mean *wolf*. Fox, Fuchs, Todd, and Volpe are all names that mean *fox*. Names such as Lyon, Lyons, Loewe, and Leon mean *lion*. And the names Buck, Hart, Hirsch, and Roe mean *deer*.

Last names such as Bird, Byrd, Crow, Crowe, Hahn, Fink, Crane, Coe, Cox, Ortega, Garza, Aguilar, Adler, and Vogel come from the word *bird* or the names of different kinds of birds.

The names Haas and Hare both mean *rabbit*. As you might guess, the name Baer means *bear*. And it might surprise you to learn that the name Drake is from the word *draca*, which means—*dragon!*

The Tale of the

Tongue

Whether you're Australian, English, Scottish, Irish, Welsh, American, Canadian, or South African, you speak English. It's a language with an exciting history! The story of how it came to be is a story of adventure, great conquests, and terrible battles. It's a tale of people traveling to new lands in search of homes. It's a story of many different languages and how they were mixed together to make the language we call English.

From grunts to grammar

How did language begin? What were the first words?
At first, there were no words. Scientists tell us
that our earliest ancestors had no language. But they
probably made noises that meant something. A growl
might have meant anger. A screech might have meant
danger. A grunt might have meant food. They probably
used gestures and made faces that meant things, too.

As millions of years passed, man's ancestors became
smarter and began to look and act somewhat like
people do today. Slowly, the first humans began to use

more and more sounds to mean things. But these
sounds weren't just noises any more—they were words.

There is no way of telling what the first real words
were. But scientists think they may have sounded
much like the noises a baby makes before it begins to
talk—sounds such as *da*, and *bo*, and *muh*.

As thousands of years passed, language grew. More
and more words were added. But there wasn't just *one*
language. There were many different languages.
Prehistoric people lived in little groups, often
hundreds of miles apart. So language grew up in many
different places—and it was different in each place.

Romans and Celts

Two thousand years ago there was no such language as English. There wasn't even a place called England.

The city of Rome, in Italy, ruled much of the world. Roman armies had conquered most of Europe and large parts of Africa and the Middle East. Finally, a Roman army invaded a large island in the North Sea off the coast of Europe—the island that now contains the country of England.

The land that is now England was then the home of tribes of people called Celts. The island was called Britannia, after the name of one of the tribes.

The Romans took over most of Britannia and ruled it for four hundred years. They built military camps,

forts, and roads, and they brought civilization to the Celts. Roman soldiers defended Britannia against the attacks of savage warriors called Picts, who lived in the northern part of the island.

Many Roman camps grew into towns and cities. In Latin, the Romans' language, the word for camp is *castra*, so many of the town names ended with that word. Later, *castra* became *caster*, *cester*, or *chester*. That's why there are many places in England with names such as Lancaster, Worcester, and Manchester. Much later, Englishmen brought some of these names to other parts of the world.

About the year 400, Rome called all the Romans in Britannia back home to Italy. When the Romans left, the story of the English language was about to begin.

The fierce warriors

The people of Britannia called themselves Britons. They spoke the Celtic and Latin languages and tried to keep up Roman customs and ways. But almost as soon as the Romans were gone from Britannia, the savage Picts from the north attacked! They invaded the lands of Vortigern, a king of the Britons.

Vortigern decided to hire warriors who were as fierce and savage as the Picts. He sent word to the Angles, Saxons, and Jutes, tribes of mighty warriors who lived about where Germany is today. Vortigern offered them land and treasure if they would help him. Soon, ships full of these hardy fighters sailed for Britannia.

The Angles, Saxons, and Jutes joined forces with the Britons. The Picts were defeated and pushed back into the north. But Britannia's troubles weren't over. The Angles and Saxons had decided to stay in Britannia and take it for themselves! More and more of these fierce warriors came to Britannia and banded together into a great army. After many years of bloody warfare, they conquered most of Britannia. It became their home.

After a while, Britannia became known as Angle-land. Slowly, that name was changed into England. The Angles and Saxons spoke the same language, which they called *Englisc*. We call that language Old English, or Anglo-Saxon. It was the beginning of the English language.

A cu, a docga, and a hus

What did the Old English language sound like 1,200 years ago? If you heard someone speaking it, you wouldn't understand what was being said. Old English sounds somewhat like German. A few words might sound familiar, but most would be strange.

Yet, a great many of the most common words we use every day come from the Old English language. The Anglo-Saxons used the words *and*, *of*, *on*, *us*, and *for*, just as we do. And many of the other words they used were words we now use, but were pronounced differently.

Here are some Anglo-Saxon words that are much like the words we use:

Anglo-Saxon	cu	docga	hus	fisc	dæg
Modern English	cow	dog	house	fish	day

The way that the Anglo-Saxons put words together
was a little different from the way we do, too.
Here is what the first line of the Lord's Prayer
looks like in Old English:

> **Fæder ure þu þe eart on heofonum,**
> **si þin nama gehalgod.**

Translated word for word, that means, "Father our,
thou that art in heaven, let thine name be hallowed."
Now that you know what each word means, you can
see that some are like words we use. *Fæder* is like
father, *ure* is like *our*, and *nama* is like *name*. But
other words are very different from words we use.

Beowulf

Beowulf is the greatest of Anglo-Saxon stories. Written in Old English, it is what is called an epic poem—a story of great adventures told in verse.

The beginning of the poem looks like this in Old English:

> **Hwæt! we Gar-Dena in geardagum,
> þeodcyninga þrym gefrunon,
> hu ða æþelingas ellen fremedon!**

These words mean, "Behold! we have heard of the glory in former years of the Spear-Danes, of the kings of the people, how the heroes did brave deeds!"

The part of *Beowulf* told here has been put into Modern English. But the words, and the ways of saying things, are very much like the story as it was first written, about twelve hundred years ago.

The poem tells how Hrothgar, king of the Spear-Danes, builds a splendid mead-hall, a building where his warriors eat and sleep. But the hall is haunted by Grendel, a hideous monster, half man and half beast, who lives in a nearby swamp. Whenever men sleep in the hall, Grendel breaks in to kill and eat some of them. The Danes are helpless against the terrible creature.

Then, from Sweden, comes a mighty warrior named Beowulf. He tells Hrothgar that he and his men will spend the night in the hall. He will fight Grendel, and either kill the monster or die himself. This is where we begin the story.

Beowulf and Grendel

Then from his head Beowulf removed the great war helmet, and from his body the coat of armor. To a follower, he gave his brave battle sword. In pride he said, "No feebler in strength am I than Grendel. I shall not destroy him with a sword. Tonight, we shall do without weapons." Then he lay down. All slept, save he. He waited for the battle-meeting.

Then, out of the misty hills, across the moor, came Grendel stalking; he that was cursed by God. 'Neath the clouds he crept till Hrothgar's hall he saw; the gaily adorned place of feasting. Though iron bars held fast the door, the monster burst them through!

The fearsome fiend entered, eager to slay; his eyes were aglow with horrid light, like fiery coals. He saw the warriors huddled there, asleep. Filled with frightful joy was he, that now he might tear the life from every man there, feasting on their blood and bones! Yet, this was not to be. Never again would he make a man victim after this night. For a mighty warrior watched to see how the man-eater made his attack.

With a sudden spring, the monster seized a sleeper,

tore open his body, bit into his bones, and devoured
him with great, greedy bites. Then, quickly, he reached
for another. But Beowulf seized his arm.

At once, the evil destroyer realized that never in
all the world had he met a man of such mighty
strength. Gone was his courage, and fear sat upon his
heart. He wished to flee, to hide in his hole in the
swamp. But Beowulf clung to him with an iron grip,
clutching Grendel till his fingers cracked.

As the two foes fought, dreadful was the din. The
warriors awakened and watched in fright the wild
battle that shook the hall. A wonder it was that the
building did not fall, so fierce was the fray as man and
monster battled. The comrades of Beowulf drew their

swords, eager to aid their chieftain. But the sharpest sword could not wound the creature.

Yet Grendel, who in other times had slain many men, felt now that his own body was breaking. Beowulf's grim grip was fierce upon him. The fearsome monster felt terrible pain. His flesh tore, the bones of his shoulder parted. With his gaping wound, Grendel escaped. He fled across the misted moor to his dark den. Well he knew that the hours of his life had come to an end. Done were his days. From the terror of the murdering monster the Danes were saved.

Beneath the high-peaked roof, Beowulf laid the token of his victory—the great, clawed arm he had torn from Grendel.

The missionaries from Rome

A little more than a hundred years had passed since the Angles and Saxons had conquered England. Everyone spoke the same language, but the country was divided into several small kingdoms, and the language was slightly different in each kingdom.

Ethelbert, king of one of the small kingdoms, was worried. His wife, Queen Bertha, was a Christian, but he was not. To please his wife, he had agreed to meet with a small band of Christian monks who had come from far-off Rome. But he was afraid of them. He had heard they were powerful magicians, and he feared they might enchant him.

The monks approached the king, carrying a large
silver cross as if it were a flag. Their leader talked to
Ethelbert and explained the meaning of the Christian
religion. As the king listened, his fears went away. He
agreed to let the monks stay in his kingdom and
preach their religion.

Soon, more and more monks came from Rome. They
spoke the Latin language, which was the language
of Rome and the language they used in their prayers
and services. In time, the people of England began to
use some Latin words. Most of the words they used
had to do with religion. And that is how words such
as altar, shrine, hymn, candle, creed, clerk, and anthem
came into the English language.

The coming of the Vikings

Thick, white fog drifted over the North Sea and the coast of England. There were no sounds except the screeches of gulls wheeling overhead and the hiss of waves rolling up on the shore.

Then, the silence was broken by the *swish-swish-swish* of oars. A fleet of long ships came sliding through the fog like lean, gray ghosts. The ships were carved and painted to look like dragons. On the ships were big, fierce warriors from the Northland. The year was 835, and the Vikings were attacking England!

For many years, England suffered terribly from the raids of the Norsemen. The Vikings sailed their ships silently along the coast, or up a river, to some

unsuspecting town. Then the warriors swarmed ashore
to burn the town and carry off all the treasure they
could find. They also carried off people as slaves.

Many of the Vikings formed together into big armies.
They conquered large parts of England and settled on
the land. There was war and bloodshed for a long time,
but the Vikings were much like the English people in
both language and custom. Soon, Norsemen and
Englishmen were living and working together, and
Norsemen were marrying English girls.

The Norse and English languages were mixed
together after a while. Many English words come from
the language that the Vikings brought to England.
Some of these words are: sky, window, skull, take,
hit, egg, skin, skirt, skill, fellow, give, get, and ugly.

The last conquest

A pale, early morning sun hung low in a gray October sky. With a clanking of armor and a clopping of horses' hoofs, the Norman army moved out to do battle against the Saxons of England.

The Normans came from Normandy, in France. Their leader was Duke William. The English king had died, and William claimed that he was supposed to be the new king. But the Saxons had made one of their leaders, Harold Godwin, king. So William had brought his army to England to fight for the crown.

Everything depended on the battle about to be fought. If the Normans won, they would rule England. If they lost, the Saxons would show them no mercy.

On a hill near the town of Hastings, the Saxons waited. For them, too, this was an all-important battle. They were fighting for their land.

The battle raged all day. But by late afternoon it was over. Harold, the Saxon king, lay dead with an arrow in his eye. The Saxons were beaten and scattered. The Normans were masters of England.

This happened more than nine hundred years ago, in the year 1066. Duke William, now known as William the Conqueror, became England's king. His men became barons and lords who ruled England under him. So, for about two hundred years all the kings and nobles of England spoke French. And, during this time, many French words became part of the English language.

New words

When you say *cow*, you're using a word from Old English. Saxon farmers who took care of the animal called it a *cu*. But when you say *beef*, you're using a word from Old French. The Norman lord who ate the *cu* for dinner called the meat *boef*.

For a long time after the Norman victory, two languages were spoken in England. The conquered Saxons spoke Old English (Anglo-Saxon). The Normans spoke Norman-French.

The Saxons were the servants and workers. This is why many of our words

for everyday things come from Old
English. The Normans were the lords and
masters. This is why many of our words
for fine food and clothing, and for law
and government, come from Old French.

The lordly Normans ate well and in
style. Some of the dining words they gave
us are fruit, soup, pork, veal, chair,
fork, napkin, and dinner. And the finely
dressed Normans also gave us the words
coat, dress, and fashion.

The Normans, of course, ran the
government and the law courts, and so
gave us such words as crown, mayor,
nation, state, judge, and justice.

The language of knights and ladies

There were castles and tournaments, knights in shining armor, and ladies in fancy gowns. Three hundred years had passed since the Normans had invaded England. People no longer called themselves Normans or Saxons—now they were all English. And they spoke a language that had slowly grown out of Old English and Norman-French. We call this language Middle English.

Middle English was much more like the kind of English we speak than was Old English. But even so, you wouldn't be able to understand much of it if you saw it written or heard it spoken. Many Middle English words are no longer used. Even those that are still used are now spelled and pronounced differently.

When we use the word *bite*, we say *byt*. But people who spoke Middle English would have said *beet* or *beet uh*. For *about*, we say *uh bowt*. In Middle English, it was *uh boot*. For done, we say *duhn*. In Middle English, it was *duhn uh*.

Middle English was spoken from about 1100 to 1500. That was a time of knights and ladies, of romance and adventure. Many wonderful poems and stories, such as those about Robin Hood and King Arthur, were first written down then.

The Canterbury Tales

This story comes from *The Canterbury Tales*,
written in Middle English by Geoffrey Chaucer.
The Canterbury Tales is a long poem that tells
of a group of religious pilgrims on their way
to the city of Canterbury, England. To pass the
time, each person tells a story. A priest tells
the story of Chauntecleer.

You would not understand many of the words
in the original. Here, for example, are the first
three lines as Chaucer wrote them in Middle
English, with the modern English words
underneath:

> **A povre wydwe, somdeel stape in age**
> (A poor widow, somewhat advanced in age)
> **Was whilom dwellyng in a narwe cotage,**
> (Was once dwelling in a small cottage,)
> **Biside a grove, stondynge in a dale.**
> (Beside a grove, standing in a dale.)

In this retelling, modern spelling has been
used. However, the sentences have been kept
much the way Chaucer wrote them, and the
expressions are much like the ones he used.

Chauntecleer and the Fox

A poor widow, growing rather old, once dwelt in a
small cottage beside a grove standing in a valley. This
widow, of whom I tell you my tale, had patiently led
a very simple life since the day her husband died. By
taking care of what God gave her, she made a living
for herself and her two daughters. She had only three
large sows, three cows, and a sheep called Moll.

94

Quite dingy was her bedroom, and also her dining room, in which she ate many a slim meal. Spicy sauces she never needed, for no dainty snacks passed through her throat. Her meals were as plain as her coat. No wine drank she, neither white nor red. Her table was set mostly with white and black—milk and brown bread—of which she had no lack. And sometimes there was broiled bacon and an egg or two.

She had a yard that was enclosed all about with a fence of sticks and a ditch. There she kept a rooster called Chauntecleer. In all the land, for crowing none was his equal. His voice was merrier than the merry organ that plays on Mass days in the church. More dependable than a clock was his crowing. The comb on his head was redder than fine coral. His bill was black, and like jet it shone. Like azure were his legs and toes, with nails whiter than the lily flowers. And like polished gold was the color of his body.

This noble rooster had in his care seven hens that were wondrously like him in color. The prettiest of these was called the fair lady Pertelote. Polite she was, careful and charming and good-natured. And truly, she had hold of the heart of Chauntecleer. He loved her well and was most happy. It was a joy to hear them sing together when the bright sun shone in spring. For in those days, so I understand, beasts and birds could speak and sing.

It happened that early one morning as Chauntecleer slept on his perch among the hens, he gave a groan deep in his throat. When Pertelote heard him she was startled and said, "Sweetheart, what ails you, that you groan so?"

And he answered, saying, "My Lady, I dreamed that I was in such trouble that my heart is filled with fear! It seemed that while I roamed up and down within our yard I saw a strange beast that was like a dog, and that tried to capture me and would have killed me. His color was a cross between red and yellow, and his tail and ears with black were tipped. He had a small snout and two gleaming eyes that looked at me so fearsomely I nearly died of fright. No doubt this frightful dream caused my groaning."

"Shame!" cried she. "I cannot love a coward, by my faith! How dare you say that anything has made you afraid? How can you have been afraid of a dream?"

"I tell you, pretty Pertelote," said Chauntecleer,

"that some dreams are to be feared. They are warnings
of things that may happen. But let us speak of happy
things, and forget all this. For, when I see the beauty
of your face, so rosy-red around the eyes, it makes
my fear die."

With those words he flew down from his perch, for it
was now daytime. He clucked whenever he found
some corn, and then the hens came running to his
call. Then, as he walked, he cast up his eyes at the sun
and knew that it was spring. Joyfully he crowed, "My
Lady Pertelote, hear how the happy birds sing, and
see how the flowers spring up. Full is my heart of joy!"

But soon he was in great trouble, for all joy ends
in sorrow.

A sly and wicked fox, with black-tipped ears and tail,
had broken through the fence in the night. And in a
flower bed he lay, waiting his chance to seize
Chauntecleer. Oh, poor Chauntecleer, this is what you
were warned of in your dream!

As Chauntecleer walked, singing, he cast his eye
on a butterfly among the flowers and saw the fox,
crouching there.

He would have fled, but the fox quickly said,
"Noble sir, where are you going? Be you afraid of me,
that am your friend? I am only here to listen to you
sing, for truly, you have as fine a voice as any angel.

"Your father, God bless his soul, and your gentle

mother have been in my house, to my delight. And I will say that, save for you, I never heard a man sing as did your father in the morning. Truly, his every song 'twas from the heart. So that his voice might be stronger, he would close both eyes and, standing on tiptoe, he would stretch his neck until it was long and thin. Now sing, Sir, and let us see if you can match your father."

Then Chauntecleer began to flap his wings, so pleased was he by all this flattery.

Ah! Take care all you great men! There is many a flatterer in your palaces, and many a trickster who cares more to fool you than he does for truth and rightness. Beware, my lords, of all their treachery!

Then Chauntecleer stood high upon his toes, stretched out his neck, closed his eyes, and began to crow with all his might. At once the fox grabbed Chauntecleer by the throat! Flinging Chauntecleer over his shoulder, he rushed back toward the woods.

Alas that Chauntecleer flew down from his perch this day! Alas that his wife paid no attention to his dream!

Great was the cry of the hens when they saw Chauntecleer carried off. And Pertelote cried loudest.

The widow and her daughters heard the noise and ran from the house. Seeing the fox heading into the woods, they ran after him crying, "Help! Help! The fox!" And after them came men with sticks, and dogs, and other women. The cows and the sows and the sheep, frightened by the barking of the dogs, ran after the men and women. Frightened geese flew up into the air and a swarm of bees came out of their hive. Such was the noise they all made, it seemed that heaven would fall down.

Now, good people, I pray you to listen. See how luck can change. For, in spite of his fear, Chauntecleer, who lay across the fox's back, did say, "Sir, if I were you I would say, 'Turn back, you interfering, ignorant clods! May a sickness fall upon you all! This rooster shall be mine in spite of you. I'll eat him, by my faith, and at once!'"

The fox answered, "By my faith, it shall be done." And the instant he opened his mouth to say this, Chauntecleer pulled his neck from the fox's teeth and broke free. Up into a tree he flew.

When the fox realized Chauntecleer was gone he said, "Oh, Chauntecleer, alas! I have done you a great wrong by frightening you when I took you out of the yard. But sir, I did not intend any wickedness. Come down, and I shall tell you what I meant."

"Nay, then," said Chauntecleer. "May I curse myself if I let you trick me more than once. Never again will flattery get me to sing and close my eyes. For he who shuts his eyes when he ought to look, may God let him never be free."

"Nay," said the fox, "but may God give bad luck to him who is so careless that he chatters when he should keep closed his mouth."

Now, you who think this is just a foolish story of rooster, hen, and fox, do not overlook the wisdom that is in it. For all that is written is written to tell some useful truth. Take the truth, and leave the rest.

The Age of Elizabeth

Spring, the sweet spring, is the year's pleasant king;
Then blooms each thing, then maids dance in a ring,
Cold doth not sting, the pretty birds do sing. . . .

You can easily understand that poem. Every word in it but one—*doth*—is a word we use today. The poem was written nearly four hundred years ago, when English was not too different from the English we speak now. England was then ruled by Queen Elizabeth I, and we call that time the Elizabethan Age.

English in the Elizabethan Age was not exactly like Modern English. There were still many differences. Some words were pronounced differently—a word such as *bite* was pronounced *bayt*. And words such as *does* and *has* were spoken and written as *doth* and *hath*. Instead of *you* and *your*, people said *thou* and *thy*.

The people of Elizabethan England were fond of plays, poetry, and music. Some of the greatest English poems and plays were written during that time. The greatest playwright of all time, William Shakespeare, lived during the Elizabethan Age. The many wonderful plays he wrote are still performed.

A Midsummer Night's Dream

William Shakespeare wrote the play *A Midsummer Night's Dream* about 1595. It is a fun-filled story about fairies, strange happenings, and enchantments.

Most of the play takes place in a woods where Oberon and Titania, king and queen of the fairies, are staying with all their elves, sprites, and goblins. A group of rather foolish men come to the woods at night so as to practice a play in secret. Shakespeare gave these men names that still make people chuckle—such names as Quince, Snug, Bottom, Flute, Snout, and Starveling.

As the men practice, a mischievous elf named Puck enchants Bottom and gives him the head of an ass, which is what a donkey was usually called in Shakespeare's time. Bottom does not know he has been enchanted. But when the other men see him they are terrified and run away.

Meanwhile, Titania, the fairy queen, has been sleeping nearby. She, too, has been enchanted so that she will fall in love with the first creature she sees when she awakens. And the first one she sees is Bottom, with his ass's head!

Here, then, is part of the play, just as Shakespeare wrote it almost four hundred years ago. Some of the words and sayings will seem strange. These have been numbered. As you come to them, you'll find them explained at the foot of the page.

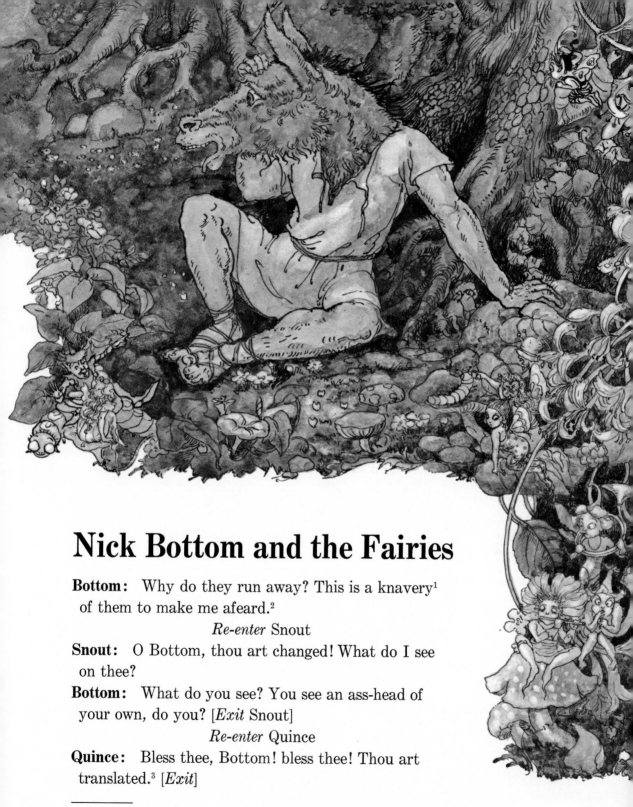

Nick Bottom and the Fairies

Bottom: Why do they run away? This is a knavery[1] of them to make me afeard.[2]

Re-enter Snout

Snout: O Bottom, thou art changed! What do I see on thee?

Bottom: What do you see? You see an ass-head of your own, do you? [*Exit* Snout]

Re-enter Quince

Quince: Bless thee, Bottom! bless thee! Thou art translated.[3] [*Exit*]

---

1. trick.   3. changed.
2. afraid.

Bottom: I see their knavery. This is to make an ass
of me; to fright me, if they could. But I will not
stir from this place, do what they can. I will walk
up and down here, and I will sing, that they shall
hear I am not afraid. [*Sings*]

> The ousel cock[4] so black of hue,
>   With orange-tawny bill,
> The throstle[5] with his note so true,
>   The wren with little quill,—

Titania: [*Awakening*] What angel wakes me from my
flowery bed?

Bottom: [*Sings*]

> The finch, the sparrow, and the lark,
>   The plain-song cuckoo gray,
> Whose note full many a man doth mark,[6]
>   And dares not answer nay;—

for, indeed, who would set his wit to so foolish a
bird?[7] Who would give a bird the lie, though he cry
'cuckoo' never so?[8]

Titania: I pray thee, gentle mortal, sing again.
Mine ear is much enamour'd of thy note;[9]
So is mine eye enthralled to thy shape;[10]

---

4. male blackbird.
5. thrush.
6. whose singing many men notice.
7. Who would bother with such a
   foolish bird?

8. Who would call a bird a liar just
   because it called "cuckoo" over
   and over?
9. I'm in love with your singing.
10. My eyes are pleased with your looks.

And thy fair virtue's force perforce doth move me[11]
On the first view to say, to swear, I love thee.

Bottom: Methinks, mistress, you should have little
reason for that. And yet, to say the truth, reason and
love keep little company together now-a-days. The
more the pity that some honest neighbors will not
make them friends. Nay, I can gleek upon occasion.[12]

Titania: Thou art as wise as thou art beautiful.

Bottom: Not so, neither; but if I had wit enough
to get out of this wood, I have enough to serve mine
own turn.

---

11. The power of your beauty moves me.   12. I can joke at times.

Titania: Out of this wood do not desire to go.
Thou shalt remain here, whether thou wilt or no.
I am a spirit of no common rate,
The summer still doth tend upon my state; [13]
And I do love thee. Therefore, go with me.
I'll give thee fairies to attend on thee,
And they shall fetch thee jewels from the deep,
And sing while thou on pressed flowers dost sleep:
And I will purge thy mortal grossness so
That thou shalt like an airy spirit go.[14]
Peaseblossom! Cobweb! Moth! and Mustardseed!

---

13. It is always summer
    in my Kingdom.

14. I will change your heavy, human body so that
    you will be like an invisible spirit.

Enter Peaseblossom, Cobweb, Moth,
and Mustardseed

Peaseblossom: Ready.

Cobweb: And I.

Moth: And I.

Mustardseed: And I.

All: Where shall we go?

Titania: Be kind and courteous to this gentleman.
 Hop in his walks and gambol in his eyes;
 Feed him with apricocks and dewberries,
 With purple grapes, green figs, and mulberries;
 The honey-bags steal from the humble-bees,
 And for night-tapers crop their waxen thighs,[15]
 And light them at the fiery glow-worm's eyes,
 To have my love to bed and to arise;
 And pluck the wings from painted butterflies
 To fan the moonbeams from his sleeping eyes.
 Nod to him, elves, and do him courtesies.

Peaseblossom: Hail, mortal!

Cobweb: Hail!

Moth: Hail!

Mustardseed: Hail!

---

15. for candles, cut off their waxy legs.

Words from everywhere

During the Elizabethan Age, the English explored the West Indies and parts of North and South America. And English merchants carried on more and more trade with the Far East. By the 1700's, English ports were crowded with ships bringing back goods, treasures—and new words—from many parts of the world.

For hundreds of years, the English language had borrowed words from other languages. Now, many more new words—for new foods, new kinds of clothing, and new animals—were brought back to England.

Sometimes these new words came straight into English. At other times the English picked them up from the French or the Spanish. On the next two pages are some of the many English words borrowed from other languages.

Words from everywhere

(continued from page 110)

Italy
balcony
bandit
carnival
piano
studio
umbrella
violin
zany

Russia
czar
mammoth

Portugal
marmalade
molasses

Spain
cigar
mosquito
tornado
vanilla

Arabia
admiral
almanac
assassin
coffee
syrup
zenith
zero

China
tea

India
bandana
bungalow
cheetah
jungle
pajamas
shampoo

Iran (Persia)
bazaar
chess
paradise
shawl
turban

Aztec Indians
chocolate

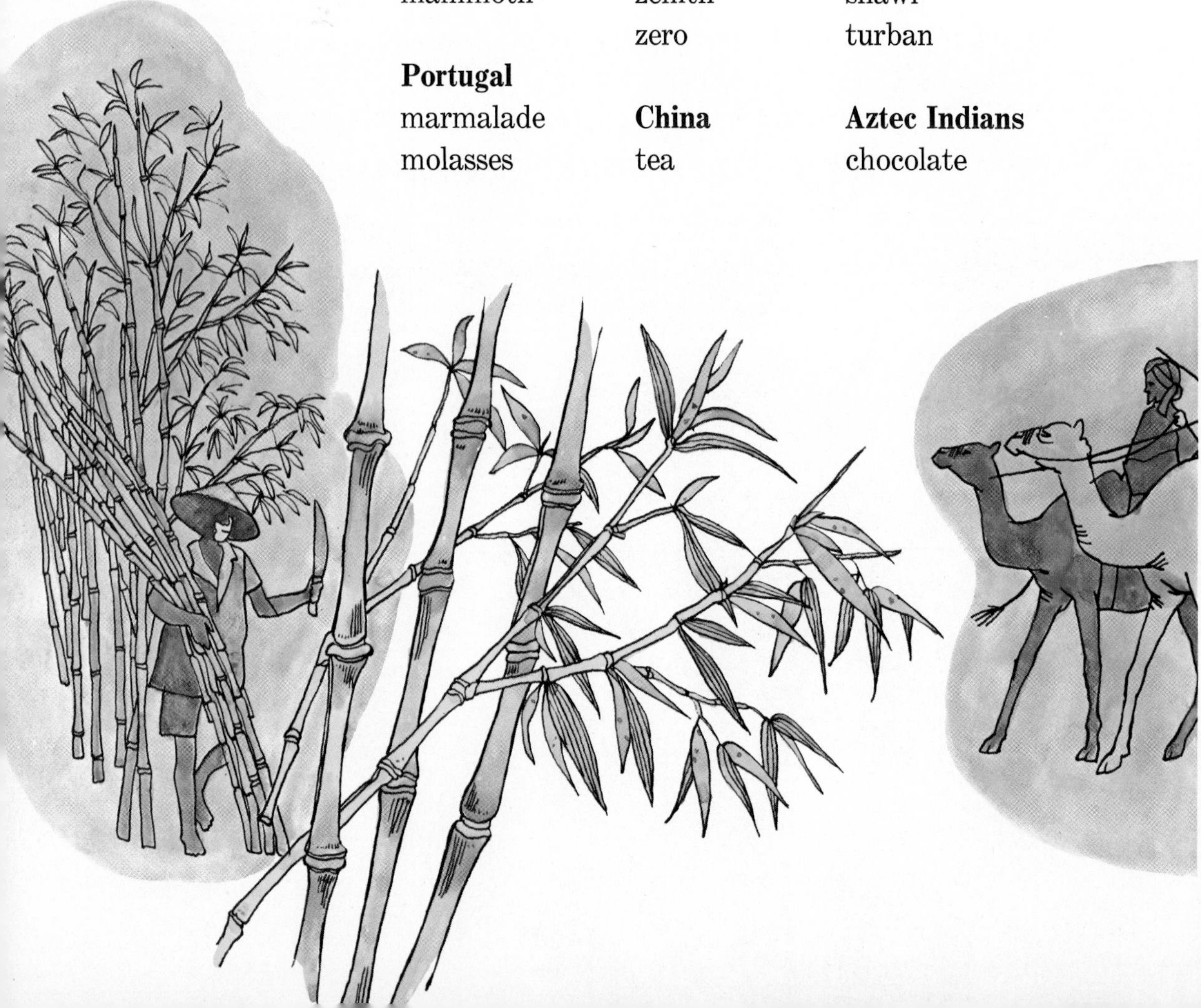

The Netherlands	American Indians	West Indies
dock	chipmunk	barbecue
skate	moccasin	cannibal
sleigh	moose	canoe
	toboggan	hammock
Africa		hurricane
voodoo	**Eskimos**	potato
zebra	igloo	tobacco
zombi	kayak	
		Malaya
Japan	**Australian Aborigines**	bamboo
judo	boomerang	gingham
kimono	kangaroo	orang-utan

By the middle of the 1800's all these words were part of the English language. People were now saying *you*, *your*, and *yours*, instead of *thee*, *thy*, and *thine*. And they no longer said *doth* and *hath* for *does* and *has*. English was very much like it is today.

A Christmas Carol

This is part of the wonderful story called *A Christmas Carol*, by the English author Charles Dickens. It was written a little more than 130 years ago. Most of the words that people used then are still used. But some of them may be new to you. When you come to a word you don't understand, look it up in a dictionary. Then you'll know a new word.

Some of the expressions that people used then are no longer used. These have been numbered. As you come to them, you'll find them explained at the foot of the page.

In this part of the story, the family of Bob Cratchit, a poor clerk, is getting ready to have Christmas dinner.

Christmas at the Cratchit's

Then up rose Mrs. Cratchit, Cratchit's wife, dressed out but poorly in a twice-turned gown,[1] but brave in ribbons,[2] which are cheap and make a goodly show for sixpence;[3] and she laid the cloth,[4] assisted by Belinda Cratchit, second of her daughters, also brave in ribbons; while Master Peter Cratchit plunged a fork into the saucepan of potatoes, and getting the corners of his monstrous shirt collar (Bob's private property, conferred upon his son and heir in honour of the day) into his mouth, rejoiced to find himself so gallantly attired, and yearned to show his linen in the

1. a dress that had been remade twice.
2. decorated with many ribbons.
3. a fine appearance, costing very little.
4. set the table.

fashionable Parks.[5] And now two smaller Cratchits,
boy and girl, came tearing in, screaming that outside
the baker's they had smelt the goose, and known it for
their own;[6] and basking in luxurious thoughts of sage
and onion, these young Cratchits danced about the
table, and exalted Master Peter Cratchit to the skies,
while he (not proud, although his collars nearly choked
him) blew the fire until the slow potatoes bubbling up,
knocked loudly at the saucepan-lid to be let out and
peeled.

"What has ever got your precious father, then?"[7]
said Mrs. Cratchit. "And your brother, Tiny Tim! And
Martha warn't as late last Christmas Day by
half-an-hour!"[8]

"Here's Martha, mother!" said a girl, appearing as
she spoke.

"Here's Martha, mother!" cried the two young
Cratchits. "Hurrah! There's *such* a goose, Martha!"

---

5. He wished to show off his clothes among the wealthy people in the parks.
6. The Cratchits, like other poor families, had no oven; the
   neighborhood baker was roasting their goose in his big oven.
7. "What has delayed your father?"
8. Martha was half an hour earlier, last Christmas.

"Why, bless your heart alive, my dear, how late you
are!" said Mrs. Cratchit, kissing her a dozen times, and
taking off her shawl and bonnet for her with officious
zeal.

"We'd a deal of work to finish up last night," replied
the girl, "and had to clear away this morning,
mother!"

"Well! Never mind so long as you are come," said
Mrs. Cratchit. "Sit ye down before the fire, my dear,
and have a warm, Lord bless ye!"

"No, no! There's father coming," cried the two
young Cratchits, who were everywhere at once. "Hide,
Martha, hide!"

So Martha hid herself, and in came little Bob, the
father, with at least three feet of comforter exclusive
of the fringe [9] hanging down before him; and his
threadbare clothes darned up and brushed, to look
seasonable; and Tiny Tim upon his shoulder. Alas for

---

9. three feet of woolen scarf, not counting the fringe.

Tiny Tim, he bore a little crutch, and had his limbs supported by an iron frame! [10]

"Why, where's our Martha?" cried Bob Cratchit, looking round.

"Not coming," said Mrs. Cratchit.

"Not coming!" said Bob, with a sudden declension in his high spirits; for he had been Tim's blood horse all the way from church, and had come home rampant.[11] "Not coming upon Christmas Day!"

Martha didn't like to see him disappointed, if it were only in joke; so she came out prematurely from behind the closed door, and ran into his arms, while the two young Cratchits hustled Tiny Tim, and bore him off into the wash-house, that he might hear the pudding singing in the copper.[12]

"And how did little Tim behave?" asked Mrs. Cratchit, when she had rallied Bob on his credulity [13] and Bob had hugged his daughter to his heart's content.

"As good as gold," said Bob, "and better. Somehow he gets thoughtful sitting by himself so much, and thinks the strangest things you ever heard. He told me, coming home, that he hoped the people saw him in the church, because he was a cripple, and it might be pleasant to them to remember upon Christmas Day, who made lame beggars walk and blind men see."

Bob's voice was tremulous when he told them this, and trembled more when he said that Tiny Tim was growing strong and hearty.

---

10. He had metal braces on his legs.
11. He had carried Tiny Tim on his shoulders, pretending to be a very fine horse, and had come home quite excited.
12. the sound of the plum pudding steaming in a large copper pot.
13. She teased Bob for believing Martha wasn't there.

His active little crutch was heard upon the floor, and back came Tiny Tim before another word was spoken, escorted by his brother and sister to his stool before the fire; and while Bob, turning up his cuffs—as if, poor fellow, they were capable of being made more shabby—compounded some hot mixture in a jug with gin and lemons, and stirred it round and round and put it on the hob to simmer; Master Peter and the two ubiquitous young Cratchits went to fetch the goose, with which they soon returned in high procession.[14]

Such a bustle ensued that you might have thought a goose the rarest of all birds; a feathered phenomenon, to which a black swan was a matter of course—and in truth it was something very like it in that house.[15] Mrs. Cratchit made the gravy (ready beforehand in a little saucepan) hissing hot; Master Peter mashed the potatoes with incredible vigour; Miss Belinda sweetened up the applesauce; Martha dusted the hot plates; Bob took Tiny Tim beside him in a tiny corner at the table; the two young Cratchits set chairs for everybody, not forgetting themselves, and mounting guard upon their posts [16] crammed spoons into their mouths, lest they should shriek for goose before their turn came to be helped. At last the dishes were set on, and grace was said. It was succeeded by a breathless pause, as Mrs. Cratchit, looking slowly all along the carving knife, prepared to plunge it in the breast; but when she did, and when the long expected gush of stuffing issued forth, one murmur of delight arose all around the board, and even Tiny Tim, excited by the

---

14. like a parade.

15. A goose dinner for the Cratchits was more rare than a black swan.

16. sitting at their places at the table.

two young Cratchits, beat on the table with the handle of his knife, and feebly cried Hurrah!

There never was such a goose. Bob said he didn't believe there ever was such a goose cooked. Its tenderness and flavour, size and cheapness, were the themes of universal admiration. Eked out [17] by the apple-sauce and mashed potatoes, it was a sufficient dinner for the whole family; indeed, as Mrs. Cratchit said with great delight (surveying one small atom of a bone upon the dish), they hadn't ate it all at last! Yet everyone had had enough, and the youngest Cratchits in particular were steeped in sage and onion to the eyebrows! But now, the plates being changed by Miss Belinda, Mrs. Cratchit left the room alone—too nervous to bear witnesses—to take the pudding up and bring it in.

Suppose it should not be done enough! Suppose it should break in turning out! Suppose somebody should have got over the wall of the back-yard, and stolen it, while they were merry with the goose—a supposition at which the two young Cratchits became livid! All sorts of horrors were supposed.

Hallo! A great deal of steam! The pudding was out of the copper. A smell like washing-day! That was the cloth.[18] A smell like an eating-house and pastrycook's next door to each other, with a laundress's next door to that! That was the pudding! In half a minute Mrs. Cratchit entered—flushed, but smiling proudly—with the pudding, like a speckled cannon-ball, so hard and firm, blazing in half of half-a-quartern [19] of ignited

---

17. added to.
18. The pudding was covered with a cloth to keep the warmth and steam in.
19. A quartern is equal to four ounces, so there was only one ounce of brandy on the pudding—a very small amount.

brandy, and bedight with Christmas holly stuck into the top.

Oh, a wonderful pudding! Bob Cratchit said, and calmly too, that he regarded it as the greatest success achieved by Mrs. Cratchit since their marriage. Mrs. Cratchit said that now the weight was off her mind, she would confess she had had her doubts about the quantity of flour. Everybody had something to say about it, but nobody said or thought it was at all a small pudding for a large family. It would have been flat heresy to do so. Any Cratchit would have blushed to hint at such a thing.

At last the dinner was all done, the cloth was cleared, the hearth swept, and the fire made up. The compound in the jug being tasted, and considered perfect, apples and oranges were put upon the table, and a shovelful of chestnuts on the fire.[20] Then all the Cratchit family drew around the hearth, in what Bob Cratchit called a circle, meaning half a one; and at Bob's elbow stood the family display of glass.[21] Two tumblers and a custard-cup without a handle.

These held the hot stuff from the jug, however, as well as golden goblets would have done; and Bob served it out with beaming looks, while the chestnuts on the fire sputtered and cracked noisily. Then Bob proposed:—

"A Merry Christmas to us all, my dears. God bless us!"

Which all the family re-echoed.

"God bless us every one!" said Tiny Tim, the last of all.

---

20. Roast chestnuts were a favorite snack.
21. the family's drinking glasses.

Explorers and Traders

Vikings

Angles, Saxons, and Jutes

Still going—still growing

The English you speak is a mixture of many languages—the Old English of the Anglo-Saxons, the Latin of the priests from Rome, the Old Norse of the Vikings, the Norman-French of the Normans, and thousands of words from all over the world.

Less than two thousand years ago there was no such thing as an English language. But today, English is

lish

Normans

Romans

Missionaries from Rome

spoken by more people than any other language except
Chinese. English is the first language of the people of
England, Scotland, Ireland, the United States,
Australia, and most of Canada. It is the official
language of Jamaica, Liberia, and Rhodesia, and one
of the two official languages of South Africa. And it
is a second language for many people in parts of Asia,
Africa, Europe, and South America. Altogether, more
than 500 million people speak English.

English

Millions of people in many parts of the world speak
English as their everyday language. But they don't all
speak it the same way. People in different places use
some different words and often pronounce words in
different ways. What kind of English do you speak?
You may be surprised to find how different your
English is from the English spoken somewhere else.

Other places, other words

The English girl said, "I'm mad about my flat!" Her American friend nodded. "I'd be angry, too, if I'd had a flat tire." But what the English girl meant was that she really liked her apartment.

The Australian boy said, "My father runs a station." His American friend thought the father ran a railroad station. But the Australian meant a sheep ranch.

At times, the British, Australians, and Americans are confused by one another's words. Sometimes, the same word means quite different things. To the British, football means a game Americans call soccer—a game quite different from American football. And sometimes the same things have different names:

British	Australian	American
plimsolls	sandshoes	sneakers
sweets	lollies	candy
galoshes	gumboots	rubbers
vest	singlet	undershirt
flat	unit	apartment

AMERICAN, BRITISH & AUSTRALIAN ENGLISH SPOKEN HERE

CANDY

SWEETS

LOLLIES

SNEAKERS

PLIMSOLLS

SANDSHOES

CHOCOLATE

People in different parts of the United States also have different names for some things. Most Americans put their groceries in a bag, but some put them in a sack and others in a poke. If you want a soft drink in New England, ask for tonic. And the sidewalk in New York is the pavement in Philadelphia.

How do you tell time? People in the Northeastern part of the United States usually say "a quarter *of* nine." In the South, people often say, "a quarter *till* nine." And in the West, many people say, "a quarter *to* nine." Which way do you say it?

At the playground, do you ride on a seesaw, tilt, teeter-totter, teeterboard, tippity-bounce, or hicky horse? Do you fish in a creek, brook, or branch?

No matter where you live, you almost certainly use some slang words. Slang is the name we give to fresh, bright words that may be made up or just used in a special way. There are slang words in every language and every country. If you say that someone is chicken —meaning afraid—you're using American slang. If you say that someone is bonkers—meaning nutty or goofy—you're using British slang. And if someone tells

Other places, other words

(continued from page 129)

you that you're his mate—meaning best friend—he's using Australian slang.

Australian English contains many slang words, as well as words from the language of the Aborigines, the native people of Australia. Here is a verse from the famous Australian song "Waltzing Matilda."

> Once a jolly swagman camped by a billabong,
>   Under the shade of a coolabah tree;
> And he sang as he watched and waited 'till
>   his billy boiled,
>   "You'll come a-waltzing Matilda with me!"

If you're not an Australian, you may not understand all the words. What's a *swagman?* What's a *billabong?*

A swagman is a wanderer—a tramp or hobo. Billabong is from an Aboriginal word meaning "branch of a river." A billy is a tin can in which the swagman boils his tea over a campfire. Matilda is not a girl, but a rolled-up blanket in which the swagman keeps his swag, or belongings. And to go waltzing means "to go for a walk or a tramp."

The people who live in one part of the city of London, England, are called cockneys. Cockneys have a special kind of rhyming slang. They may say "trouble

and strife" instead of *wife*, "plates of meat" for *feet*, "apples and pears" for *stairs*, "loaf of bread" for *head*, or "mince pies" for *eyes*. This kind of slang is even harder to understand when it is shortened, so that *loaf* stands for *head* and *minces* for *eyes*.

What do you say when you want someone to go away? An American might say "Get lost!" or "Bug off!" But a cockney would say " 'Op it!"

Slang is always changing. About eighty years ago, if an American were asked to do something he didn't want to do, he'd probably have said, "Not on your tintype!" Forty years ago he might have said, "Not a chance!" Recently the expression heard most often was "No way!" What will it be next?

Slang makes language very colorful and interesting. But too much slang "covers up" the language and makes it hard for people to understand one another. And there is no point in telling someone to " 'Op it!" if he or she doesn't understand what " 'Op it!" means!

How to spell fish

Do you think you know how to spell *fish?* Well, think again. We usually spell a word by the sounds in the word. But English is full of different letter combinations that have the same sounds. If you listen to the sounds in *fish* and remember the wrong letter combinations, you might end up with *ghoti!*

Impossible? Not at all. Take the *f* sound of *gh* in *enough* (*ih nuhf*), the *i* sound of *o* in *women* (*wihm uhn*) and the *sh* sound of *ti* in *nation* (*nay shuhn*) and you get ghoti, not fish. Can you think of strange ways to spell other words?

There was a time when people spelled words just about any way they wanted to. But it is easier if we all spell words the same way. This is one reason for

dictionaries. But even with dictionaries, we still don't all use the same spelling for many words.

If you're a bookworm, you may have found this out for yourself. The fact is, the British and Americans spell some words quite differently. And Australians and Canadians use many British spellings. Here are a few examples of the differences in British and American spellings you may see in books:

British	American	British	American
centre	center	gaol	jail
colour	color	defence	defense
tyre	tire	cheque	check
connexion	connection	plough	plow
kerb	curb	draught	draft
waggon	wagon	aluminium	aluminum

Other places, other sounds

How do you say the word *again?*

How you say it depends on where you live or how you've learned to say it. Most people in Canada and the United States say *uh gehn.* But in the New England States, many people say *uh gan.* In the Southern States, most people usually say *uh gihn,* as do many people in Scotland and Ireland. Many people in England say *uh gayn.* But in parts of England and Australia, some people say *uh gyn.*

The way people say words is part of what is called dialect. Most people call it accent. We say that someone speaks with a Southern accent, or an English accent, or whatever kind of accent. We usually think of *other* people as having an accent. But everyone speaks with some kind of accent.

There are three main accents in the United States. The most common accent is called General American. This is what you hear in most of the West, the Midwest, and parts of the East. If you go to the South or Southwest, you will hear a Southern accent. And in the Northeast, you will hear a New England accent. Within these areas you will also hear other accents.

About three out of four Americans have a General

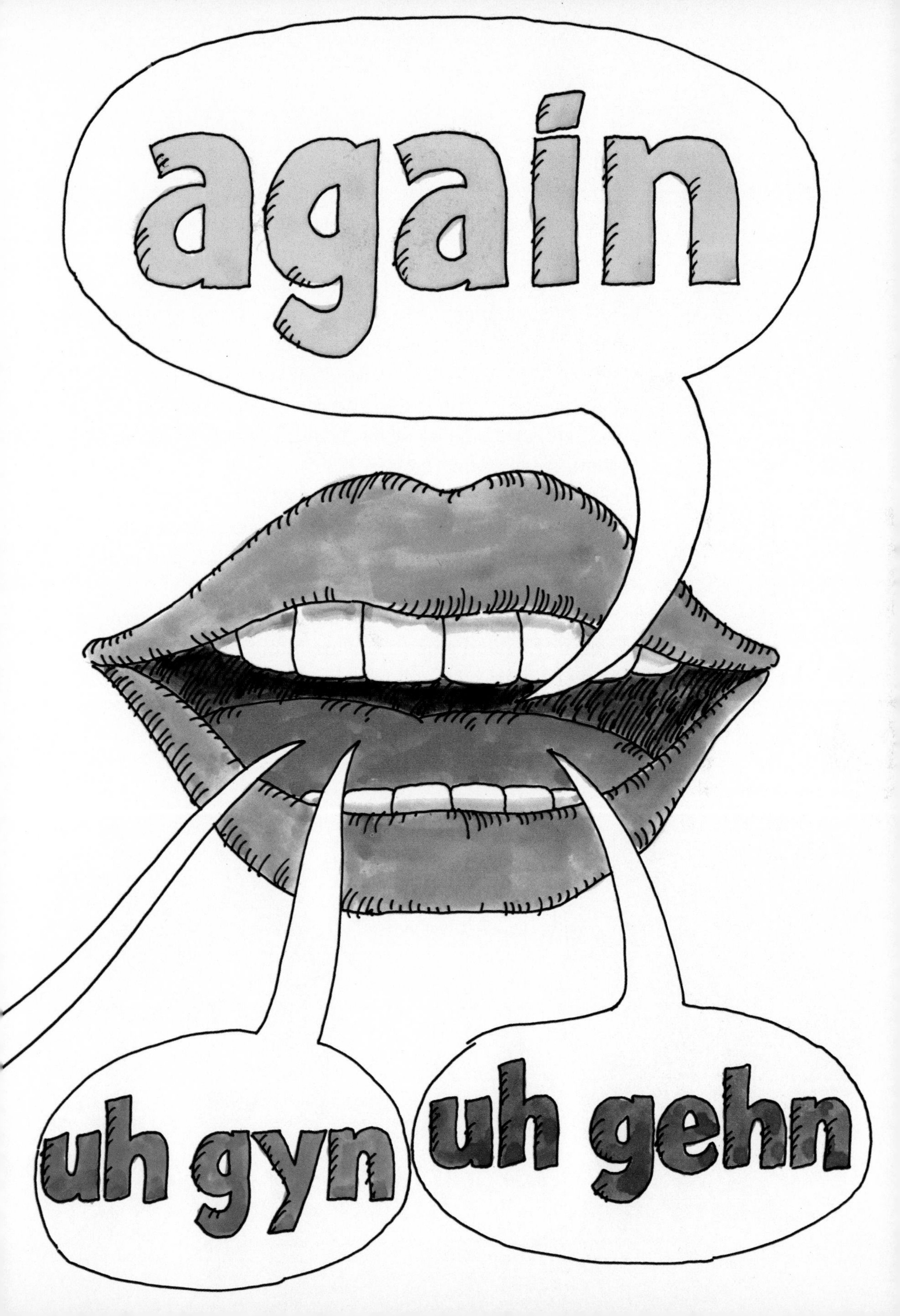
again
uh gyn
uh gehn

Other places, other sounds
(continued from page 134)

American accent. In this accent, the *r* is always heard. Most Americans say *bawrd* for *board*. But many New Englanders say *bawd* and most Southerners say *bohd*.

New Englanders often speak with a broad *a*, so that many words have an *ah* sound. They say *fahst* for *fast* and *pahth* for *path*. They also drop the *r* sound, pronouncing *farm* as *fahm* and *car* as *cah*. And if a word ends with an *ah* or *aw* sound, they often use an *r* sound, saying *sawr* for *saw*.

In the South and Southwest, most people have a Southern accent. They stretch out vowel sounds and drop their r's. They say *suh* for *sir*, *Ah* for *I*, and *doah* for *door*.

In Great Britain, there are some two dozen dialects. Even in England alone there are many dialects. For the word *heart*, you will hear *hurt* in Lancashire, *hawrt* in Devonshire, *hairt* in Northumberland, and *ahrt* among the cockneys of London. How do you say the

words *clerk, schedule,* and *vitamin?* Many people in Great Britain and Canada say *klahrk, shehd yool,* and *vih tuh mihn.* But most people in the United States say *klurk, skehj ule,* and *vy tuh mihn.*

A person who speaks with a strong Australian accent says *lydee* for *lady, iht* for *hit,* and *dy* for *day.* When you hear Australians say, " 'Owyergoin'mateorright?" they mean "How are you going (doing) mate (pal), all right?" And in New Zealand, people seem to say *uht uhz* for *it is.* Many people in Canada speak with an accent that is much like General American. But Canadians may give an *oo* sound to words that have *ou* in them. They often say *oot* for *out* and *aboot* for *about.*

So, what kind of accent do you have? How do you say *log* and *dog,* or *cot* and *caught,* or *marry, Mary,* and *merry?* When you say the word *greasy,* do you say *greesee* or *greezee?* When you ask for a drink of water, do you ask for *wawter* or *wahter?* Try listening to yourself and others. You will soon discover many differences in the way people say words.

Other languages, other sounds

When people from other countries learn English, their way of speaking often sounds strange to us. They use many of the sounds from their language in place of English sounds. This causes them to speak English with different accents.

People from Germany and Austria often pronounce such English words as *wind* and *water* with a *vee* sound instead of a *wuh* sound. So they say *vind* and *vater*. This is because there is no *wuh* sound in German. Germans pronounce the letter *w* as *v*. Germans have no *th* sound either—they pronounce *th* like *d*. So, when they speak English, they say *dihs* and *daht* for this and that.

In Spanish and Italian, the letter *i* is pronounced with an *ee* sound. So, Spanish-speaking and Italian-speaking people give an *ee* sound to the *i*'s in English words. If a person from Spain or Italy or Mexico says, "this is a big ship," you may hear "thees ees a beeg sheep."

Just as there are different sounds in every language, so there are different ways of saying things. Sometimes, a person learning English seems to get things mixed up. Instead of saying, "I had to cross the street," they might say, "I had the street to cross." This is because that's the right way to say it in their language. To them, "I had to cross the street," is bad grammar!

It's not easy to learn another language. So don't make fun of people who speak English with what you think is a strange accent. They should really be admired. They're doing something that's very difficult!

From Sounds to

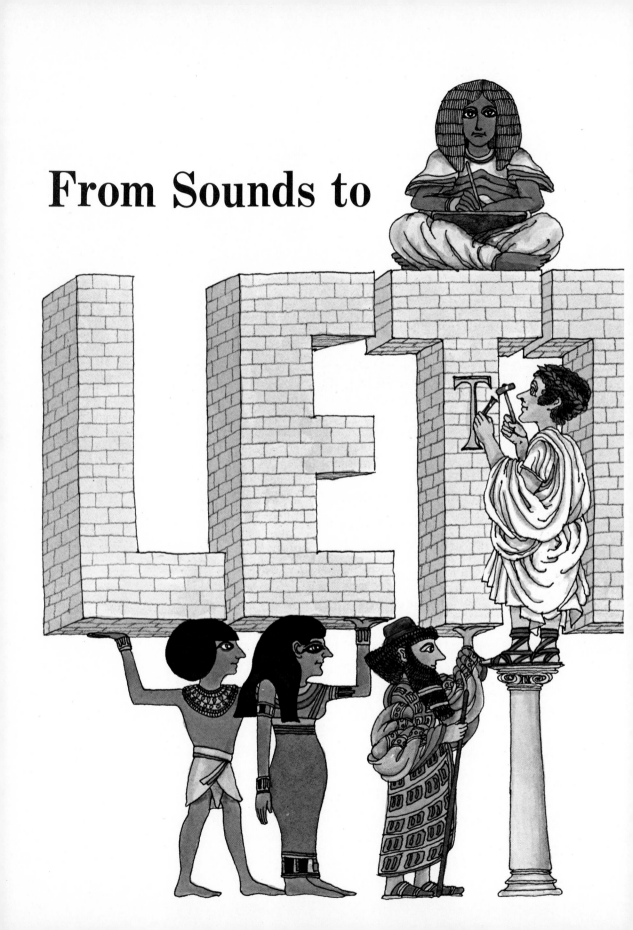

People once made pictures that stood for words. That was the start of writing, about five thousand years ago. About two thousand years later, people learned to use pictures to stand for sounds. That was the beginning of the alphabet. Writing and the alphabet were two of the greatest of all inventions. Here's how they came about.

Marks in mud

Writing began as pictures drawn in lumps of mud!

We didn't always have writing. For hundreds of thousands of years, the only way people could pass ideas along was by talking. There was no way to write stories or keep written records. So people had to do a lot of remembering.

Then, about five thousand years ago, in a hot land in the Middle East, someone had a wonderful idea. Pictures could be used to stand for spoken words. With rows of pictures that stood for words, people could put down stories, send letters to each other, and keep historical and business records.

Pictures that stand for words are called pictographs. This word simply means "picture writing." The first people to use pictographs were the Sumerians who lived

144

Sumerian picture writing

Marks in mud

(continued from page 143)

about where the country of Iraq is today.
The Sumerians must have had a hard
time finding pictures for some of their
words. It's easy to turn a word such as
fish, *bird*, or *house* into a picture—you
just draw a picture of a fish, a bird, or a
house. But it's not so easy to find pictures
for words such as *here*, *understand*, or
good. Try it and see.

The Sumerians solved this problem by
putting different pictures together to
mean certain words. For example, their
picture for the word *food* was a bowl,
because they ate out of bowls. When they
put a picture of a head next to a tilted
bowl, it meant *eat*. But there is a big
problem with this kind of writing. You
need *lots* of pictures—one picture for
almost every different thing or idea.
Early Sumerian writing probably had

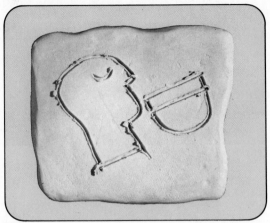

Sumerian picture writing for the word "eat"

more than two thousand different pictures!

The Sumerians made their pictures with sharp sticks in flat lumps of clay. This clay wasn't like the modeling clay you use. It was more like thick, stiff mud! The clay tablets were covered with pictures and then baked or dried in the sun. This made them hard.

If you have tried to draw pictures in clay, you know it isn't easy. It's especially hard to draw curves. The lines get filled in and the edges get squeezed up. This happened to the pictures the Sumerians made on their clay tablets. But since clay was the best thing the Sumerians had to write on, they had to put up with it.

However, after a time, the Sumerians found that it was easier to draw only straight lines. So they began to make all their picture words out of straight lines.

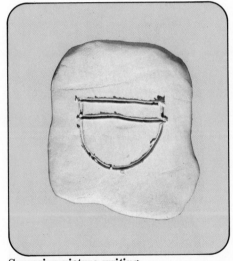

Sumerian picture writing for the word "food"

(continued on page 146)

cuneiform tablet and writing stick

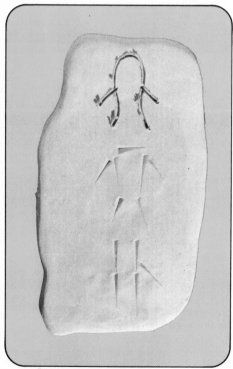

three ways to write fish

First, the word was a picture.
Then, the picture was
made with straight lines.
Finally, it became a symbol.

Marks in mud
(continued from page 145)

For example, the word *fish* was first a
picture of a fish made with curved lines,
then it was made with straight lines, and
finally it became a bunch of straight
lines that didn't look like a fish at all.
Then it was no longer a picture word. It
was a symbol that stood for a word. All
the Sumerian writing became symbols
that stood for words or parts of words.

The way the Sumerians pushed their
little sticks into the clay caused the
marks to look like golf tees. So, instead
of being all straight lines, the Sumerian
writing began to look like designs made
with golf tees.

This kind of writing is called cuneiform,
which means "wedge-shaped." For more
than two thousand years, the cuneiform
writing started by the Sumerians was
used by Assyrians, Babylonians, and
other people in the same part of the
Middle East.

Assyrian cuneiform writing of 2,800 years ago, on a stone carving

Sumerian cuneiform writing of about 4,400 years ago

The language detective

How is it that we are able to read the strange-looking cuneiform writing of the Sumerians? No one has spoken their language for thousands of years. How can a language be read if no one knows what the symbols mean?

We learned this language mainly through the work of a man who studied, and puzzled, and put clues together until he figured out how to read cuneiform writing. His name was Henry Rawlinson.

Rawlinson was a British army officer. In 1835 he was on duty in Persia, which is now called Iran. While there, he visited Behistun Rock, a cliff in the Persian countryside. High up on this rock there is an ancient carving of a king, his servants, and a group of

Behistun Rock

prisoners. And there are three different kinds of ancient cuneiform writing.

Rawlinson copied the cuneiform inscriptions and began to study them. He realized that one of them was in a language much like an East Indian language that he could speak and write. Slowly, he worked out the meaning of this inscription, which was in ancient Persian. It told of the deeds of Darius, king of Persia.

Rawlinson then found that the names of some kings in the Persian inscription seemed to be repeated in the other inscriptions. Perhaps all three inscriptions said the same thing! Using the Persian inscription as a key, Rawlinson was able to puzzle out the meanings of the symbols in the other inscriptions. Thanks to the work of Rawlinson and others, we are now able to read the cuneiform writing invented in ancient Sumer.

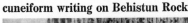

cuneiform writing on Behistun Rock

Gilgamesh

This is part of the legend of Gilgamesh, one of
the oldest stories in the world. It was told by
the people of Sumer, Babylon, and Assyria
thousands of years ago. Indeed, it may be the
first story ever written down. When we learned
to read cuneiform we discovered this wonderful
tale, which had been lost to the world for more
than two thousand years.

The Journey of Gilgamesh

In the land of Sumer, in the city of Uruk, there lived
two great and mighty warriors. One was Prince
Gilgamesh, son of Queen Ninsun. The other was
Gilgamesh's dearest friend and constant companion,
Enkidu.

Gilgamesh was a happy, carefree young man. But
one day he awakened filled with gloom. He spent most
of the day deep in thought. Then he went to see his
friend.

"Enkidu," he said, "all men die, and someday I, too,
will die and be gone from the world forever. My name
will be forgotten. It will be as if I had never been!
I cannot let this happen. I must do something to make
my name live on. So, I am going to the Mountain of
the Cedar Forest that is the home of the evil monster
Humbaba. I will challenge the monster to fight me.

When I have killed him, I will put my name on a stone and set the stone on the mountaintop."

Enkidu raised his hands in alarm. "You do not know what a terrible creature this Humbaba is," he cried. "His breath is fire and a whirlwind! His footsteps are earthquakes! The gaze of his eye turns men to stone!"

"What does it matter?" argued Gilgamesh. "If I am to die anyway, I may as well die battling this creature. Then, men will always remember that I died bravely!"

Enkidu sighed. "I will go with you, of course," he told his friend. "But I beg of you to pray to Shamash the sun god and ask for his help."

So Gilgamesh prayed to the sun god, telling him what he planned to do and asking his help.

"When you are in need, I will help you," whispered the voice of Shamash.

Then Gilgamesh and Enkidu went to the metalworkers and had their swords and axes sharpened. When the wise men who governed the city of Uruk heard of Gilgamesh's plan they raised their hands in horror and pleaded with him not to go. His mother, Ninsun the queen, wept and wrung her hands. She, too, prayed to Shamash to protect her son and help him come safely back.

Gilgamesh and Enkidu set out. For many days they traveled. They crossed mountains and made their way through dark forests that seemed to go on forever. But at last they reached the foot of the Mountain of Cedars. It rose above them, tall and awesome, its peak lost in the clouds.

Then Gilgamesh grasped his ax and with several blows brought one of the trees crashing to the ground. The sound of its falling echoed on the mountainside.

Far up in the cedar forest there was a terrible roaring, like the sound of a whirlwind. Out of his house of cedar logs stalked the monster Humbaba. He was taller than three men, with arms and legs as thick as tree trunks and great claws on his fingers and toes. His mouth was filled with sharp teeth. In the middle of his forehead was one eye, the eye whose glare could turn men to stone.

The ground shook and the cedar trees shuddered as the monster strode down the mountainside. Gilgamesh and Enkidu gripped their weapons and waited.

Humbaba burst out of the trees and bent his head to look down upon the two men and turn them to stone. But at that moment, burning winds and a fierce brightness came out of the sky and struck Humbaba's eye so that he howled with pain and covered his eye with his hand. The sun god, Shamash, was helping Gilgamesh in his time of need, as he had promised.

At once, Gilgamesh and Enkidu leaped to the attack. They slashed the monster's legs so that he tumbled to the ground, and at once they cut off his head. Then Gilgamesh and Enkidu returned to Uruk in triumph.

The goddess Ishtar, who had seen the terrible battle,
fell in love with the handsome Gilgamesh. Appearing
beside him, she put her hand on his arm and smiled at
him. "Gilgamesh," she said, "be my husband! Marry
me. As a wedding present I will give you a chariot
made of gold and covered with jewels. I will enchant
your horses so that they are the swiftest and your oxen
so that they are the strongest. I will make all the
kings and rulers of the world bow down before you!"

Ishtar was gloriously beautiful, but Gilgamesh
frowned and shook off her hand. "If I marry you,
what will become of me?" he asked, quietly. "It is
known, O Ishtar, that you have had many husbands.
When you tire of one, you turn him into a dog or a

snake! Why should I let such a thing happen to me? No, I will not marry you."

Ishtar's beautiful face turned hideous with rage. She rushed up to heaven and appeared before her father, Anu, the father of all the gods. "Gilgamesh has insulted me," she hissed like a snake. "Punish him! Set loose the mighty Bull of Heaven to trample him and gore him!"

"If I let loose the Bull of Heaven, terrible things will happen to the world of men," Anu warned. "There will be storms of wind, raging floods, and starvation."

"I will hold back the winds and floods, and see that the people do not starve," shrieked Ishtar, "but I want Gilgamesh punished! Set loose the Bull!"

So Anu loosed the Bull. It came rushing down out of

heaven, bellowing with the sound of thunder and shaking its horns so that lightning flashed. The breath from its nose sent whirlwinds rushing before it, and the force of its hoofs made the earth shudder with earthquakes as it smashed the gates of Uruk.

But when the Bull charged at the two heroes, Enkidu seized it by the horns and held it still while Gilgamesh buried his ax in its neck and killed it.

Ishtar appeared again. "Woe to you, Gilgamesh!" she shrieked. "You have insulted me and killed the mighty Bull of Heaven. I will have vengeance upon you!"

The two friends simply laughed at her. They cut up the Bull and divided it among the people. Then Gilgamesh went to give thanks to the sun god.

ancient Egyptian hieroglyphics

Pictures on paper

The Sumerians put down stories and kept records in cuneiform. But, at this same time, people in other parts of the Middle East and Asia were also working out ways of writing.

The people of ancient Egypt invented a kind of picture writing we call hieroglyphics. This name means "priestly carvings." The Greeks gave it this name because they thought the Egyptian priests were the only ones who used and understood this kind of writing.

Egyptian picture writing looks nicer than the picture writing of the Sumerians. Egyptian hieroglyphics are made up of charming pictures of people, animals, birds, plants, and everyday things with which the Egyptians were familiar. At first, each picture stood for one thing. Later, the pictures stood for words or parts of words.

The ancient Egyptians also gave the world something better to write on than clay. They invented paper! To make sheets of paper, they used the dried leaves of the papyrus plant. These plants grew thickly along the banks of the Nile, the great river that flowed through their land. The Egyptians left many records on sheets of papyrus paper, often in several different colors. They also carved their hieroglyphics on stone monuments and painted them in bright colors on the walls of tombs and temples.

Some Egyptian writing was in straight lines, as ours is. But the Egyptians wrote the lines from right to left, like this

.esuom a desahc tac ehT

And some Egyptian writing went from top to bottom and right to left, like this

a	c	T
	h	h
m	a	e
o	s	
u	e	c
s	d	a
e.		t

hieroglyphics on a statue

Words from ancient Egypt

When you set in the western horizon of heaven
The world is in darkness like the dead . . .
Every lion comes forth from his den
The serpents they sting. Darkness reigns . . .

Bright is the earth when you rise in the horizon . . .
The two lands are in daily rejoicing,
Awake and standing upon their feet . . .
Then in all the world they begin their work.

Those lines are from an ancient Egyptian hymn to
the sun, written more than three thousand years ago.
The Egyptians wrote hymns, poems, and stories in
their hieroglyphics. We can read these words from

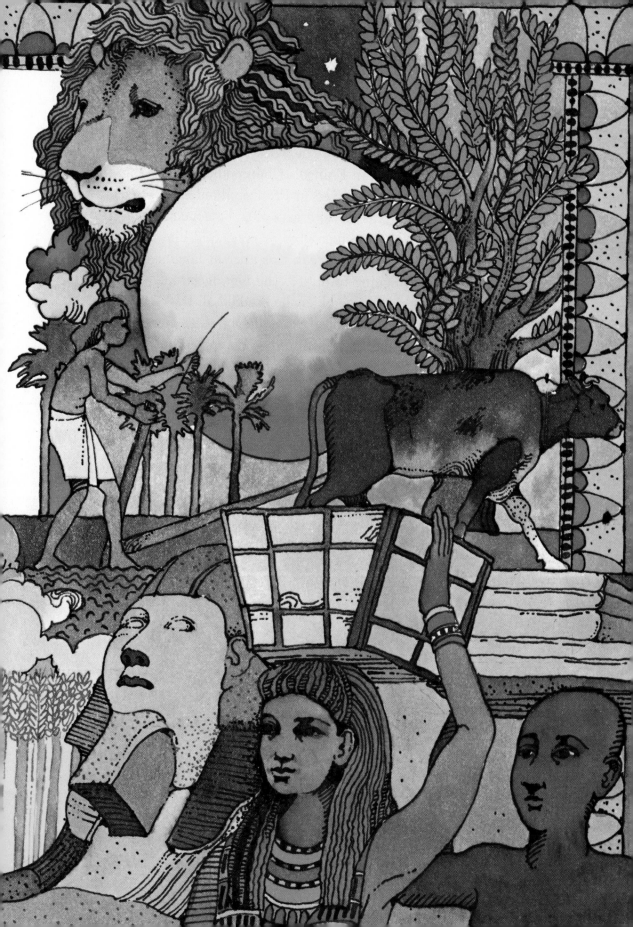

Words from ancient Egypt
(continued from page 160)

long ago because of the work of another language
detective, Jean François Champollion.

Champollion lived in France, about 150 years ago.
When he was eleven years old, someone showed him
some Egyptian hieroglyphics and told him that no one
in the world could read this ancient language.

"I am going to do it!" the boy declared.

When he grew older, he studied all that was known
about hieroglyphics. He made copies of hieroglyphic
writing that had been found. He sorted out all the
different kinds of pictures that were used in them. And
he learned to speak several ancient languages.

In 1799, a French soldier in Egypt found a large stone slab with three kinds of writing carved on it. This stone was named the Rosetta Stone. Some of the writing on it is in ancient Greek and some is in hieroglyphics.

Ancient Greek was one of the languages that Champollion had learned. When he saw the stone, he noticed that in the Greek writing several names were repeated. Then he found some of the hieroglyphics were repeated in just the same way. Perhaps the Egyptian hieroglyphics said the same thing the Greek writing did. In time, he was able to match the hieroglyphics to the Greek. He had solved the mystery of Egyptian writing, just as he said he would!

the Rosetta Stone

The wonderful invention

It takes us only a few seconds to write the words, "I wonder." But here's how an Egyptian wrote them:

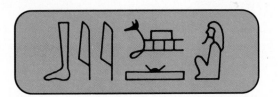

One of the problems with both hieroglyphic and cuneiform writing was that it took a long time to write anything. Most words were made up of several pictures or symbols, and each one took time to draw.

Another difficulty was that hundreds of pictures or symbols were needed. The earliest cuneiform writing had about six hundred symbols, and hieroglyphics also used several hundred symbols. In both kinds of writing, a symbol could stand for a word or a syllable. Only men who had spent years learning the meanings of all

these pictures and symbols, and how to make them, could write. It took so long to learn how to write, and the writing seemed so hard to do, that most people thought it was a kind of magic.

Then, about 3,500 years ago, came a wonderful invention—the alphabet! The people who had this great idea lived in a land of brown hills and palm trees, between where Egypt and Israel are today. We call these people Semites. They were probably slaves of the Egyptians, but their invention of the alphabet changed the world.

At first, the Semites probably used Egyptian writing, with its hundreds of pictures. But wise men among the Semites must have realized that a picture could stand for a single sound just as well as for a word or a syllable. They began to use some of the Egyptian symbols for sounds. This made it faster and easier to write. Finally, they had twenty-two sound-symbols that could be put together to make any word in their language. This was the beginning of the alphabet.

(continued on page 166)

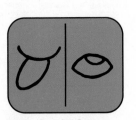

these Semite letters
stood for sounds we
don't use in English

Semite letters on an ancient coin

The wonderful invention
(continued from page 165)

Each symbol was a picture of something, and stood for the first sound in the name of the thing pictured. For example, a wavy line, which was a picture of water, was called *mem*, the Semitic word for water. But to the Semites the symbol *mem* didn't *mean* water. It stood for the first *mm* sound in the word *mem*.

Two of the symbols used by the Semites, an ox head and an eye, stood for scratchy, growly sounds we don't have in English. Several others stood for sounds we make by putting two of our letters together, such as *ts* and *sh*. And all the Semitic letters stood for hard sounds such as *kuh* and *tuh*, the sounds we call consonants. The Semitic alphabet had no letters for sounds such as *ay*, *ee*, and *oh*, the sounds we call vowels.

On the next page is a make-believe Semitic ABC that shows the shapes and names of their letters. A word in our language shows the sound each Semitic letter stood for. Perhaps this should be called a BGD, because *B*, *G*, and *D* are the first three letters shown. Two of the letters, the ox head and the eye, have been left out. We don't use the sounds they stood for.

The alphabet
goes to sea

When the alphabet was invented,
people called Phoenicians lived along the
coast of what is now Israel and Syria.
They were skillful sailors, brave explorers,
good craftsmen, and clever businessmen.
Their ships glided through the sparkling
waters of the Mediterranean Sea,
exploring the shores and islands. When
the Phoenicians found people, they offered
to trade brightly colored cloth, jewelry,
and spices for whatever valuable things
the people might have.

Phoenician alphabet

Phoenician lettering

The Phoenicians didn't live far from where the alphabet was discovered, so they soon heard about this new way of writing. Before long, they began to use it themselves. They spoke much the same language as the inventors of the alphabet, so they didn't need to change any of the sounds the symbols stood for. But they did change the shapes of most of the symbols—perhaps to make them easier to write.

The Phoenicians took their new writing to sea with them, to use for keeping records of their business deals. Thus, the alphabet was carried to other lands.

New sounds and shapes

The Phoenician traders often sailed across the Mediterranean Sea to a land of purple mountains and dark green groves of olive trees. This land was called Hellas by its people. Today, we call it Greece.

There is a legend that a Phoenician prince named Kadmus taught the Greeks the alphabet. But before the Greeks could use it, they had to make changes.

For one thing, the Phoenician language was nothing at all like the Greek language. Some sounds the Phoenicians used, the Greeks didn't use. For another

New sounds and shapes

(continued from page 170)

thing, the Phoenician alphabet had only consonant sounds, but the Greeks needed seven vowel sounds. So the Greeks used some of the Phoenician symbols for different sounds and added several new symbols for new sounds. They also changed the shapes of many of the Phoenician symbols to ones they liked better.

The Greeks called the first two letters of their alphabet *alpha* and *beta*—and that's where our word *alphabet* comes from.

Greek alphabet

Greek lettering carved on stone

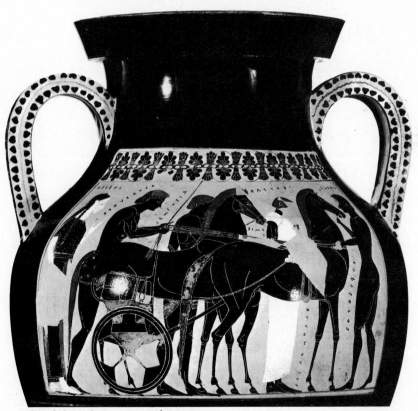

Greek lettering on an ancient vase

More changes

Just as the Phoenician alphabet traveled to Greece, the Greek alphabet traveled to other places, too. About 2,700 years ago, a rich, powerful people called Etruscans ruled much of northern Italy. They used the Greek alphabet, with a few changes to meet the needs of their language.

One of the places the Etruscans ruled was a simple farming community called Rome, whose people called themselves Romans. In time, the Romans rose up and drove out the Etruscans. But the Romans kept many of the good ideas they'd gotten from the Etruscans, such as paved streets, sewers, laws, and the alphabet.

Over a period of time, the Romans, too, made changes in the alphabet. For one thing, they put in a letter that looked like our *v*, but they used it for both the vowel sound of *u* and the consonant sound of *w*.

(continued on page 176)

Roman lettering carved on stone

More changes

(continued from page 174)

They didn't need a *zee* sound, so they took the letter *z* out. Later, they put it back in to use for foreign words. But they put it at the end of the alphabet.

The Romans also changed most of the Greek letters into shapes with neat, straight lines and curves. By about two thousand years ago, their alphabet looked much like ours does now, except that it did not have the letters *j*, *u*, or *w*.

The Romans called their list of letters the *alphabetum*.

Roman coin with lettering

Roman alphabet

2,000 years of the alphabet

Semite alphabet

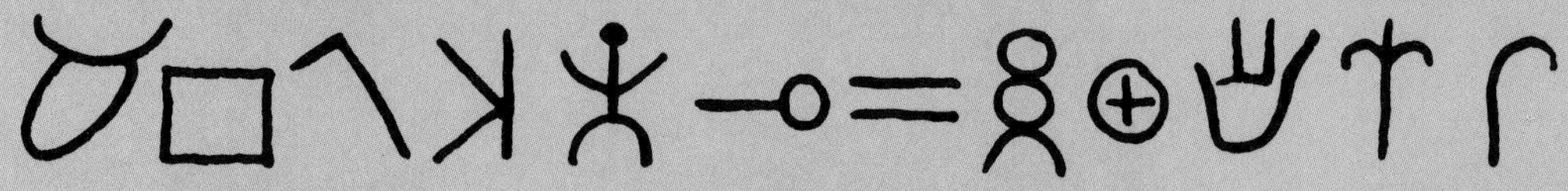

Phoenician alphabet

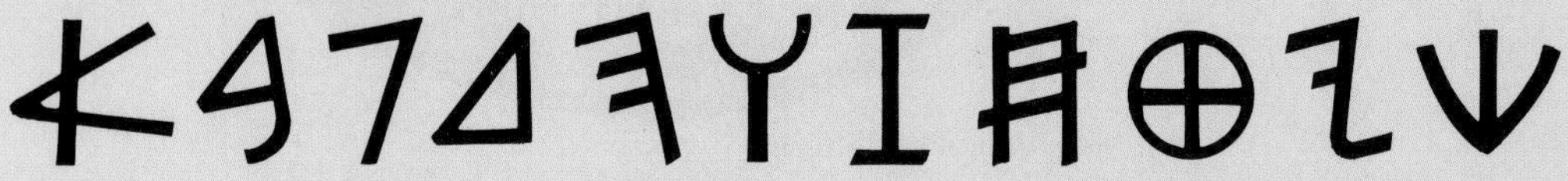

Greek alphabet

ABΓΔEZHΘIKΛMNΞ

Roman alphabet

ABCDEFGHIKLMNOP

ΟΠΡΣΤΥΦΧΨΩ

QRSTVXYZ

Little letters

Rome began as a tiny village, but grew to be a great city and the capital of a huge empire. The Romans conquered much of Europe, Britain, Greece, and parts of North Africa and the Middle East. They spread their language and alphabet into many of these places.

Much Roman writing was carved on stone buildings and monuments. The alphabet used for stone carving was made up of the kinds of letters we call capitals.

But some writing was done with feather pens and ink on parchment, which is a kind of thick, stiff paper made of sheepskin. In time, the shapes of the capital letters were changed so that they were easier to make with a pen. This new writing was called cursive script.

About 1,200 years ago, some French priests began to make a Bible that was written entirely by hand, on parchment pages. The priests wanted the book to be as beautiful as possible, so they changed the Roman cursive script letters into shapes they thought were prettier. And to save time and space, they made the letters smaller. This was the beginning of the little letters—called lower-case letters—that we use today.

Roman capital letters carved on the Arch of Titus in Rome about 1,900 years ago

Aram autem . genuit aminadab · Aminadab
autem . genuit Naasson ; Naasson autem . genu
it salmon · Salmon autem . genuit booz de ra
chab ; Booz autem . genuit obed ex ruth · Obed
autem . genuit iesse ; Iesse autem . genuit da
uid regem ; Dauid autem rex . genuit salomo
nem ex ea quae fuit uriae ; Salomon autem .
genuit roboam · Roboam autem . genuit abia ;
Abia autem . genuit asa · Asa autem . genuit
iosaphat ; Iosaphat autem . genuit iora · Iora
autem . genuit oziam ; Ozias autem . genuit
ioatham · Ioatham autem . genuit achaz ;
Achaz autem . genuit ezechiam · Ezechias au
tem . genuit manassen ; Manasses autem . genu
it amon · Amon autem . genuit iosiam ; Iosias
autem . genuit iechonia & fratres eius · in trans
migrationem babilonis ; Et post transmigrati
onem babilonis. iechonias genuit salathiel ;
Salathiel autem . genuit zorobabel · Zorobabel
autem . genuit abiud ; Abiud autem . genuit elia
chim · Eliachim autem . genuit azor ; Azor autē .
genuit sadoc · Sadoc autem . genuit achim ; Achim
autem . genuit eliud · Eliud autem . genuit eleazar ;
Eleazar autem . genuit matthan · Matthan
autem . genuit iacob ; Iacob autem . genuit ioseph
uirū mariae. de qua natus ē. ihs. qui uocatur xps ·

lower-case lettering done in France almost 1,200 years ago

The story of *w* and *u*

Why do we call *w* "double *u*"? It's made out of two *v*'s—*vv*—so it's really a double *v*, not a double *u*.

Until about nine hundred years ago, there was no *w* in the English alphabet. There was, however, a letter that looked somewhat like a *p* and was used for the sound *wuh*. In 1066, French-speaking people called Normans conquered England. The Normans brought monks with them to do most of their writing. Of course, the writing was in French, but the monks often had to use English words. This was sometimes a problem because the Normans had no letter for the *wuh* sound.

The monks solved the problem with their letter *v*, which they used for the vowel sounds *oo* and *uh*, as well as for the consonant sound *vee*. The *wuh* sounded like *oo-uh* to the monks, so they pushed two *v*'s together —*vv*—to make a new letter for the *oo-uh* sound. But because they wrote their *v* either as *v* or *u*, they often wrote the new letter with two *u*'s—*uu*. They called the letter "double v," but in English it became "double u."

Hundreds of years later, Italian printers began to use *v* only for the consonant sound *vee*, and *u* for the vowel sounds *oo* and *uh*. Thus, *u* came into the alphabet, making twenty-five letters. Only one more letter was needed to make the alphabet the way it is today.

A dot and a tail

When the French monks made a lower-case *i*, it had no dot. It looked like a stubby *l*. When one of these *i*'s stood next to an *l*, it was easy to confuse the two letters for an *h*. And when two *i*'s were used side by side, as they often are in Latin, they could be mistaken for *n* or *u*. About five hundred years ago, printers in Venice, Italy, solved this problem. They made an *i* with a dot over it. And we have been putting dots over our lower-case *i*'s ever since.

But there was still sometimes a problem when two *i*'s were used together. They might look like two *l*'s. To solve this problem, a tail was often added to the second *i*, like this—*ij*. Later, an *i* at the beginning of a word was also written with a tail.

In those days, the letter *i* stood for two sounds.

One was the vowel sound *eye* that we give it now. The other was a consonant sound like *yuh*. But about four hundred years ago, Spanish printers began using *i* for the vowel sound and *j* for the consonant sound. English printers quickly borrowed this idea. They used *j* for the *juh* sound we give it now, and put it into the alphabet right after i. And that is why our alphabet now has twenty-six letters.

With those twenty-six letters we speak to each other silently in hundreds of ways—with books, magazines, newspapers, signs, and many other things. These letters have been turned into raised dots that blind people can feel and into shapes that deaf people can make with their fingers. Letters have also been turned into clicks, buzzes, flashes of light, and flags for sending messages. The alphabet is perhaps the greatest of all inventions!

Aa

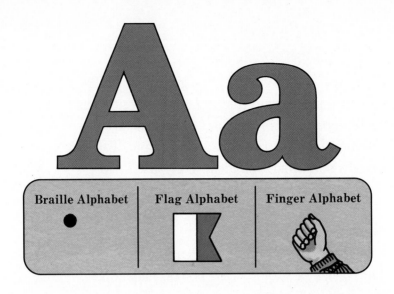

Braille Alphabet	Flag Alphabet	Finger Alphabet

an **A**ngry **a**ardvark **A**larming an **a**ddled **A**lligator

Bb

Braille Alphabet	Flag Alphabet	Finger Alphabet

a **B**ashful **b**ear **B**ehind a **b**are **B**lueberry **b**ush

Cc

Braille Alphabet	Flag Alphabet	Finger Alphabet

a **C**arefree **c**hubby **C**at in **c**olorful **C**ircus **c**lothes

Dd

| Braille Alphabet | Flag Alphabet | Finger Alphabet |

a **D**elighted **d**inosaur **D**evouring a **d**elicious **D**inner

Ee

| Braille Alphabet | Flag Alphabet | Finger Alphabet |

an **E**nergetic **e**lephant **E**ntertaining **e**legant **E**els

Ff

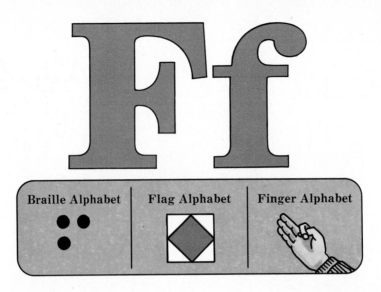

Braille Alphabet	Flag Alphabet	Finger Alphabet

a Frightened fish Fleeing from a Ferocious foe

G g

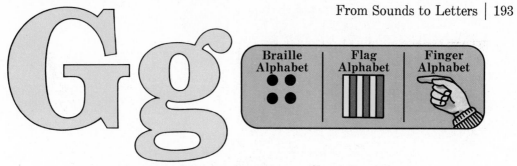

Braille Alphabet	Flag Alphabet	Finger Alphabet

a **G**orgeous **g**ang of **G**leefully **g**rinning **G**enies

H h

Braille Alphabet	Flag Alphabet	Finger Alphabet

Hungry **h**amsters **H**appily **h**auling a **H**uge **h**am

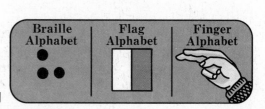

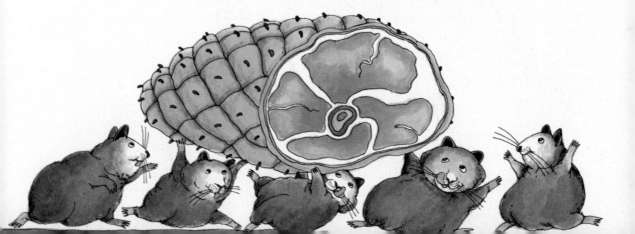

Ii

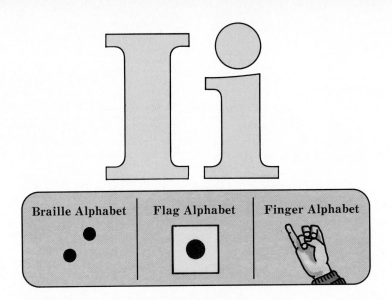

| Braille Alphabet | Flag Alphabet | Finger Alphabet |

an **Icy** impresario **Instructing impudent Insects**

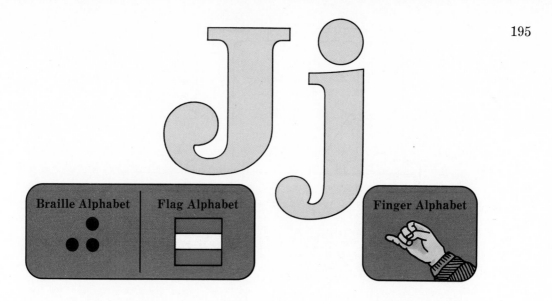

Braille Alphabet | **Flag Alphabet** | **Finger Alphabet**

Jovial jabberwocks Jesting in a jumbled Jungle

Kk

Braille Alphabet	Flag Alphabet	Finger Alphabet

a **K**indly **k**angaroo **K**nitting a **k**nobby **K**eepsake

Ll

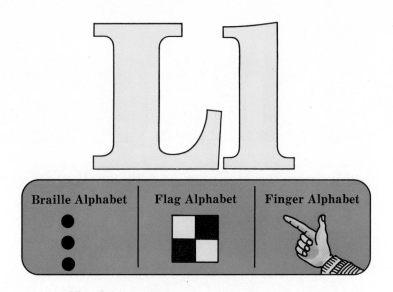

Braille Alphabet	Flag Alphabet	Finger Alphabet

Lazy lizards Lying in a littered Lair

Mm

Braille Alphabet	Flag Alphabet	Finger Alphabet

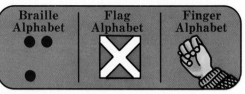

a **M**oody **m**onster **M**oaning on a **m**isty **M**ountaintop

Nn

Braille Alphabet	Flag Alphabet	Finger Alphabet

a **N**earsighted **n**ightingale **N**apping in a **n**eat **N**est

O o

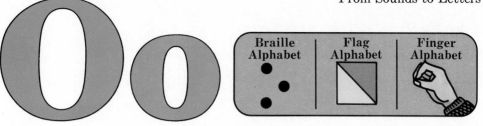

| Braille Alphabet | Flag Alphabet | Finger Alphabet |

an **O**verweight **o**ctopus **O**gling **o**rnate **O**ysters

P p

| Braille Alphabet | Flag Alphabet | Finger Alphabet |

a **P**arty of **p**rim **P**igs **p**ompously **P**icknicking

Braille Alphabet | Flag Alphabet | Finger Alphabet

a **Q**uarrelsome **q**ueen **Q**uashing a **q**uaking **Q**uintet

Rr

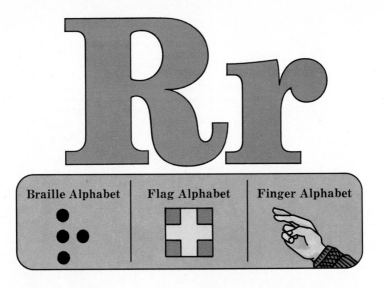

Braille Alphabet	Flag Alphabet	Finger Alphabet

a **R**otund **r**hinoceros **R**elentlessly **r**educing

Ss

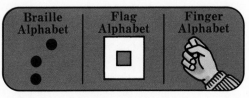

Braille Alphabet | Flag Alphabet | Finger Alphabet

a Stylish skunk Seated on a short Stump

Tt

Braille Alphabet | Flag Alphabet | Finger Alphabet

a Tidy tiger Timidly taking a Tedious trip

Uu

Braille Alphabet | **Flag Alphabet** | **Finger Alphabet**

an Unlucky uncle Under a useless Umbrella

Vv

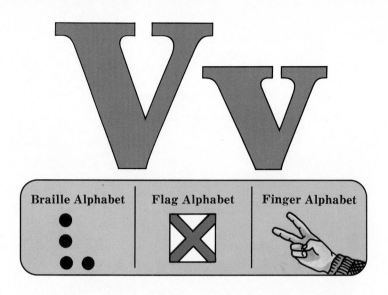

| Braille Alphabet | Flag Alphabet | Finger Alphabet |

a **V**ain **v**ampire **V**iewing a **v**acant **V**ault

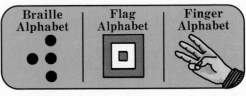

| Braille Alphabet | Flag Alphabet | Finger Alphabet |

a Wealthy worm Wearing a weighty White wig

| Braille Alphabet | Flag Alphabet | Finger Alphabet |

an eXuberant ox eXamining an extraordinary Xylophone

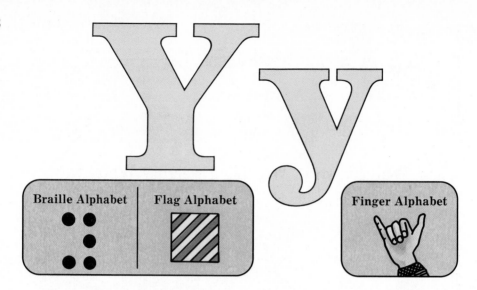

Braille Alphabet **Flag Alphabet** **Finger Alphabet**

Yacking young Yaks in a yard of Yellow yams

Zz

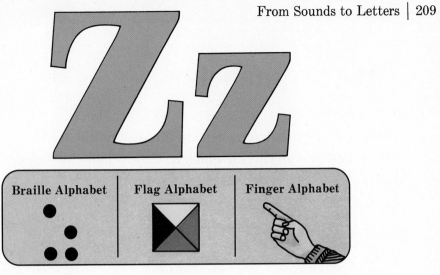

Braille Alphabet	Flag Alphabet	Finger Alphabet

a **Z**ealous zebra **Z**igzagging a **Z**any zeppelin

Other alphabets

Almost all languages have an alphabet. But the alphabets of other languages are often very different from ours, just as the Phoenician, Greek, and Roman alphabets were all different.

Gaelic alphabet

ⱥ b c ꝺ e ꝼ ᵹ h ı l m n

Hebrew alphabet

תשרקצצפפעסנממלדכי

Russian alphabet

АБВГДЕЖЗИЙКЛМНОПР

opkstu

אבגדהוזחט

СТУФХЦЧШЩЪЫЬЭЮЯ

People Who Work with

"Word jobs" are important. People who work with
words give us books, magazines, plays, newspapers,
television and radio programs, and many other things.
Perhaps, some day, you'll decide to write stories, or
poems, or plays. Or you may want to study language
and teach it to others. The next few pages will give you
an idea of some of the ways you can work with words.

Creative writers

A writer's job seems simple. People think that all a writer needs is some paper and a pen, pencil, or typewriter. Because writing looks easy, many people try to make money writing. However, to succeed, a writer must have something to say—something people want to read or hear about. And, whatever is written must be written in an interesting way. Good writing is hard work.

All writers are creative, whether they are poets or newspaper reporters. But the term "creative writer" usually means certain kinds of writers—those who write stories, poems, or plays.

Writers who write storybooks are called novelists. Those who write plays are called playwrights, or dramatists. And someone who writes poetry is a poet. There are also those who write articles for magazines or scripts for radio, television, or the movies. Of course, some creative writers do many kinds of writing.

How does a writer get started with a book, a play, a magazine article, or a poem? Well, first, there must be an idea. Writers usually get ideas from things they see or hear or read. As a rule, getting the idea is the easiest part of writing.

The next thing a writer has to do is find out as much as possible about everything that has to do with the idea. This finding out is called research. What does a writer look for? All kinds of things. Where does he or she look? All kinds of places. Getting information may mean going to libraries and museums or traveling to distant places. It almost always means talking to people and asking questions.

Once the research is done, a writer must study and

researching for a book

Research is an important part of any book. This author checks facts at a museum and also talks to young readers to find out what interests them.

Creative writers
(continued from page 215)

organize the information. Some writers make an outline. They put down the main ideas, in order, and then arrange the information under those ideas.

The actual writing is the hard and lonely part of working with words. Few writers are happy with their first draft, or try at writing something. Most make many changes and write several drafts. Each draft brings them closer to what they want to say in the way they want to say it.

People who write for television and the movies must

key the words to the pictures. And the author of a
play must take into account the size of the stage, the
skills of the actors, and the scenery that might be
used. Poets have still other problems, for they use
words to produce rhythm and rhyme. For a poet, the
sounds of words are often just as important as the
meanings of words.

Some writers write three thousand or more words a
day. Others may take a week to write that much.
Some writers use pencil and paper, others a typewriter.
And some start with pencil and paper and do the later
drafts on a typewriter.

Finally, there comes the day the writer is finished.
If the work is a book, article, or poem, it is usually
sent to a book or magazine editor. If it is a play or
a script for television, radio, or the movies, it is
usually sent to a person called a producer. If the
editor or producer likes it, he will buy it. Then,
someday, you will have a chance to read or hear the
writer's words.

making changes in a story

A writer usually makes many
changes in a first draft, or
try at writing something.

Reporters

A reporter's job is to get the news and write it in an interesting way for a newspaper.

Reporters have many ways to find out what's happening. They keep in touch with police and fire departments and with city and state governments. People also telephone news to the newspaper or write letters. And many groups send information about what they are doing.

When a reporter goes out on a story, he or she interviews people to find out what happened and what the people saw or heard. The reporter also looks around carefully to get descriptions of everything.

If time is short, the reporter phones the information to the paper. Then another person writes the story. When there is more time, the reporter comes back and types the story at his or her desk. But reporters must work fast. There is always a deadline for each day's paper.

Reporters also check and double-check their facts. The important facts—the answers to *who, what, why, where, when,* and *how* always appear near the beginning of a story. Then, if the story is cut, or shortened, to fit the space, no facts are lost. Reporters must stick to the facts. Good reporters do not put opinions —what they think—into news stories.

calling a story in

talking to people at the scene

Editors

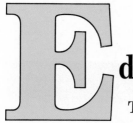

There are many kinds of editors. In some ways their jobs are alike. They check facts, spelling, and grammar. They also check to see that stories and articles are interesting and read well. But in other ways their jobs are very different.

Magazine editors choose the subjects of the articles to be published. They assign writers to research and write articles. They hire photographers to take pictures and artists to draw illustrations. And they decide what issue an article goes into. They want to be sure that there is good variety in each issue.

Book editors always look for good writers. One way they do this is to read the stories people send to them. If a story is good, they may arrange to buy it. If they don't like it, or can't use it, they send it back. Book editors also suggest ideas to authors. They work with the author while he or she is writing the book. When the writing is finished, the editor works with the artists, designers, printers, salespeople, and others who help to make and sell the book.

A newspaper editor decides if a story belongs on page one or in the middle of the paper. He or she also decides how much space to give a story. And, quite often, the editor writes the headline.

magazine staff planning an issue

checking proofs of color pictures

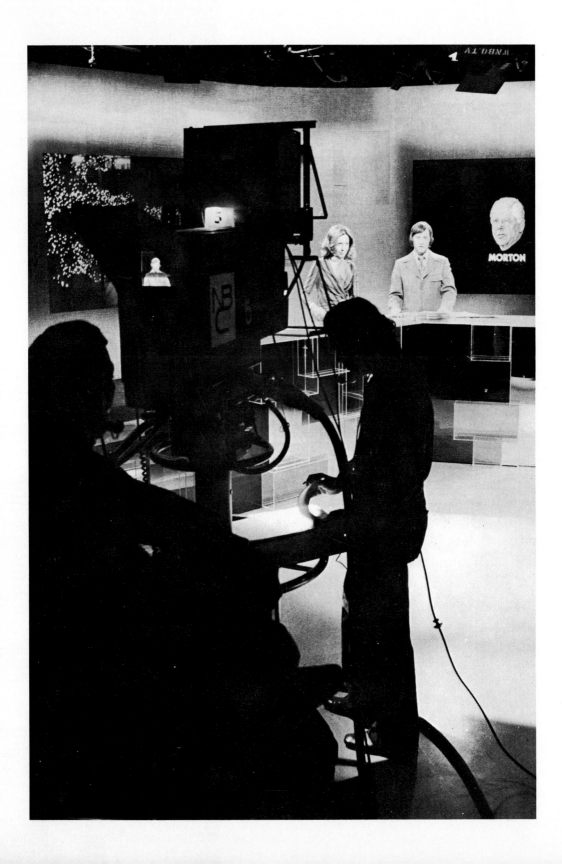

Newscasters

Newscasters report the news on television and radio. But, unlike newspaper reporters, newscasters use the spoken word. We *hear* their words instead of reading them.

The newscaster you hear may work for a local station in your town or city, or for a nationwide broadcasting company. Some newscasters do on-the-spot, or "live," broadcasts. Others film and taperecord interviews and events all over the world. The video and sound tapes are then sent to the studio, where they are cut to fit the time available.

Newscasters deal with the sounds of words as well as their meanings. They look for good-sounding words. Sometimes they use slang or jargon—the bright, fresh words of athletes, astronauts, and others. This is how many new words and expressions become part of our everyday language.

The men and women who broadcast the news also influence the way we speak. Most of them speak without strong accents. As a result, people in different parts of the United States are slowly losing their different ways of saying words. The same thing is happening in Canada, Great Britain, and Australia.

broadcasting the news

taping and filming an interview

Copywriters

People who write the words, or copy, for the advertisements and commercials you read and hear are called copywriters.

Copywriters must be able to put ideas into words. They try to think of new and catchy ways to describe things. They also have to think about the pictures and sounds that will go with the words.

Most copywriters work for advertising agencies. When preparing advertisements or commercials, the copywriter talks over ideas with an art director. The copywriter then writes the copy and the art director sketches pictures.

For a printed advertisement, words and pictures are put together in a layout. For a television commercial, a storyboard is made. A storyboard is like a cartoon strip. It has pictures, words, and directions for sound effects.

The layout or storyboard must then be checked by the people paying for the ad. When approved, it goes into production. This is when it is made ready to go to newspapers, magazines, television or radio stations, or outdoor sign makers.

Good advertising gets your attention, holds your interest, and makes you want what is advertised. The next time you read an ad or hear a commercial, see if the words do these things.

planning a new advertisement

going over a storyboard

ord scientists

Have you ever wondered how to find the best words with which to say or write something? Or where a word comes from? Or why we don't all say a word the same way?

People who are interested in these things are called linguists. A linguist is a "word scientist." Linguists work at answering questions about language.

There are more than 600,000 words in the English language. Each year, some words go out of style and other words enter the language. Keeping track of these words, which ones are used most, and their changing meanings is the job of people called lexicographers. This name comes from two Greek words and means "writer of wordbooks." Lexicographers write lexicons, or books of words. We call these books dictionaries.

The first English dictionary was published almost four hundred years ago. Early English dictionaries were usually the work of a single person. But today,

learning the shapes and sounds of letters

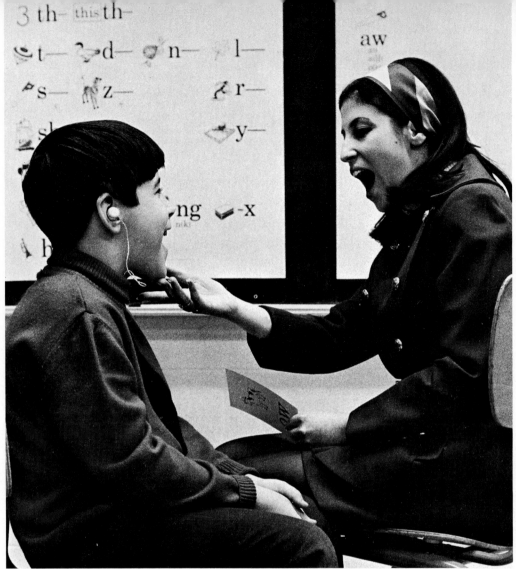

speech therapist helps a child to sound a word

Word scientists

(continued from page 227)

lexicographers have large staffs to help them with
their work. There are also people all around the world
who send them examples of how words are being used.

Other linguists trace the history of words. These
people are called etymologists. This name comes from
a Greek word that means "the very first form of a
word." Etymologists want to find out how and when a
word came into the language. They also show us how

word meanings change. Has anyone ever called you an imp? Nowadays, imp means "naughty child." But its first meaning was "young shoot of a plant."

Some linguists study the ways in which languages are alike. These men and women discovered that languages that seem as different as English, French, German, Russian, Greek, and Persian are really related languages. Many of the simple words in these languages are very much alike. For example, the English word *mother* is *mère* in French, *Mutter* in German, *mat'* in Russian, *meter* in Greek, and *mader* in Persian. The reason the words are alike is that these languages all come from the same "parent" language.

We call this parent language Indo-European. It was spoken some five to six thousand years ago. That was before the invention of writing, so there are no written words in this language. But, by studying related languages, linguists now know many Indo-European words. They have also learned that the people who spoke this language lived about where Germany and Poland are today. And from there, the Indo-European language spread across Europe and part of Asia—west to Ireland and east to India.

We learn what these word scientists have learned from another kind of word scientist—the English teacher. English teachers show us how to use our language correctly and help us to get the most out of it. Other teachers, called therapists, aid children who have speech and reading problems. These teachers go through special training so that they can do this kind of work.

Do you think you would like to work with words? If so, perhaps someday you will be a writer, an editor, a newscaster, or a word scientist.

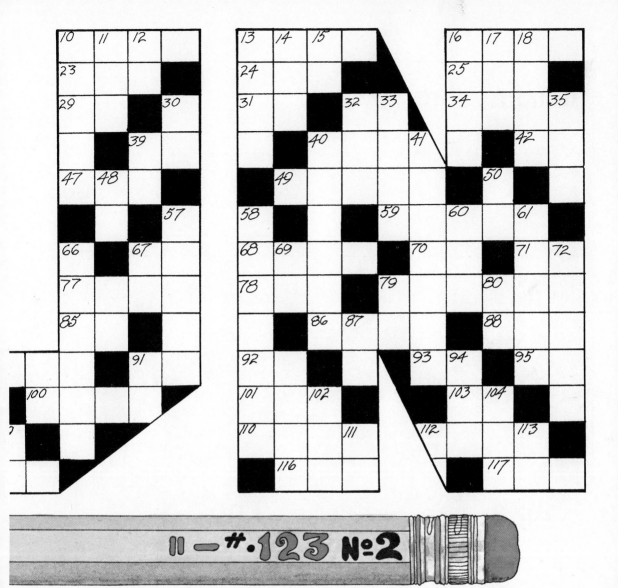

with Words

Did you ever stop to think how many games, puzzles, and other ways of having fun depend on words? Here's a collection of riddles, tongue twisters, crossword puzzles, puns, and many other kinds of word games. See for yourself how much fun you can have with words! And how much you can learn while having fun.

Read a rebus

Say the word for each picture and you have read a
rebus. A rebus is a puzzle with pictures for some words.

Sometimes a rebus uses a letter of the alphabet for a word. Read the letter aloud, and it sounds like a word.

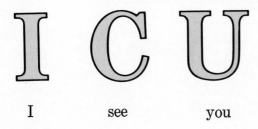

I   see   you

Other letters sound the way some people say words.

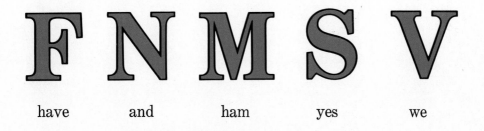

have   and   ham   yes   we

Using only letters, here's how you would write "Have you ham and eggs?":

F U M N X ?

Here's how you would write "Yes, we have ham and eggs.":

Read a rebus
(continued)

Here are some two-letter combinations that sound like words. Just read the letters aloud, quickly:

EZ NE AT MT

easy   any   eighty   empty

Jack Spratt and his wife "licked the platter clean," so their platter was—MT.

A rebus may also use a number for a word:

$$1 \quad 2 \quad 4 \quad 8$$

won   to, two, or too   for   ate

The 2 hungry rats 8 the cheese. The hungry cat 8 the rats. A number can also be part of a word:

$$1 + \text{derful} = \text{wonderful}$$
$$10 + \text{t} = \text{tent}$$

Read a rebus
(continued)

You can also use the words *on*, *in*, *over*, and *under* to make rebus words.

The letter P is **on** the letter Y.
So, p + on + y spells pony.

Let's try another one. The picture tells the answer.

C
E

This Bible character was swallowed by a big fish.

The letter K is **in** the letter G.
So k + in + g = king.

What's this girl's name in a famous fairy tale?

What green vegetable is this?

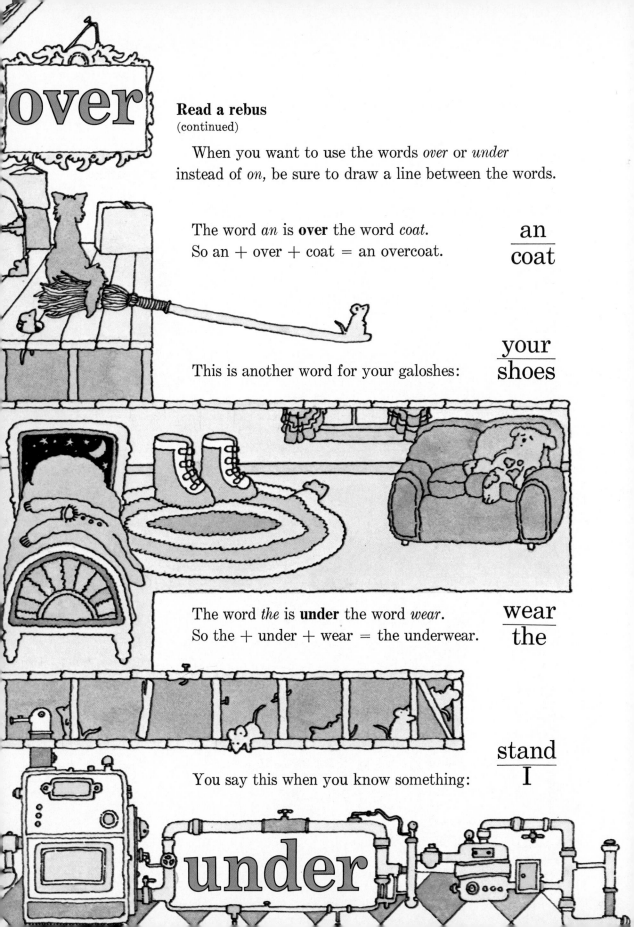

over

Read a rebus
(continued)

When you want to use the words *over* or *under* instead of *on*, be sure to draw a line between the words.

The word *an* is **over** the word *coat*.
So an + over + coat = an overcoat.

$$\frac{an}{coat}$$

This is another word for your galoshes:

$$\frac{your}{shoes}$$

The word *the* is **under** the word *wear*.
So the + under + wear = the underwear.

$$\frac{wear}{the}$$

You say this when you know something:

$$\frac{stand}{I}$$

under

You can mix words, letters, pictures, and numbers to
make a rebus. From what you've learned, can you read
this rebus?

Across

Down

1				2			
				3			
4							
5			6				

1

2

Crossword puzzles

Trace these puzzles on a sheet of thin paper. Be sure to mark in the numbers, as shown.

In the rebus puzzle above, what does each picture stand for? Think of the word, then print the word in the box with the number that matches the picture.

In the crossword puzzle on the next page, find a word that fits the spaces for the listed clues.

Across

1. ____sauce
6. Student
7. Rebus letter for *have*
8. First two letters of 9 across
9. Girl's name
11. River in Italy
13. There
14. They help you glide over snow.
15. An abbreviation for "Thomas"
16. Post office abbreviation for "Land of Lincoln"
17. Opposite of *he*
18. Upon
19. Abbreviation for *company*

Down

1. Large monkeylike animal without a tail
2. Jack-o'-lantern
3. Peter Pan's initials
4. Not to tell the truth
5. A tree
7. Dad
10. Short for *mathematics*
12. Cars use gas and ____.
14. Rebus letter for *yes*
17. For that reason
18. Zero
19. Roman numeral for 100

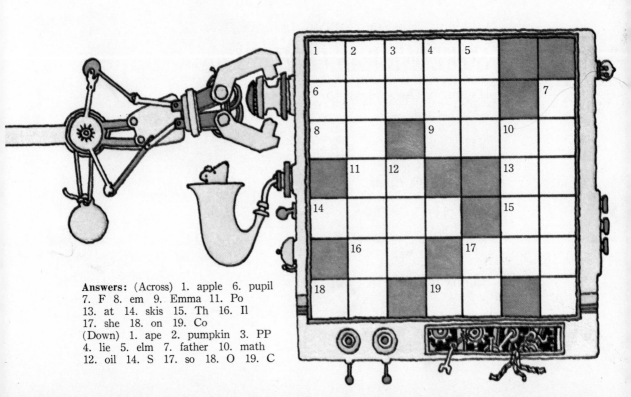

Answers: (Across) 1. apple 6. pupil
7. F 8. em 9. Emma 11. Po
13. at 14. skis 15. Th 16. Il
17. she 18. on 19. Co
(Down) 1. ape 2. pumpkin 3. PP
4. lie 5. elm 7. father 10. math
12. oil 14. S 17. so 18. O 19. C

The Riddle of the Terrible Sphinx

The horrible monster lay on a rock near the top of the mountain.

It waited, silently.
Who would be its next victim?

This terrible beast was the Sphinx. It had the head of a woman, the body of a lion, the wings of a bird, and the tail of a serpent. The Sphinx had eaten hundreds of people on their way to the nearby city of Thebes. And all because these people could not answer the riddle the cunning Sphinx had asked them.

Suddenly, the Sphinx *raised* its head.

SOMEONE WAS COMING!

Its sharp claws began to

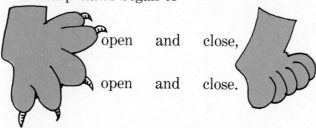

open   and   close,

open   and   close.

A man drew near. He was about to pass, when the Sphinx *leaped* in front of him.

"I will let you pass safely," the Sphinx said, *"if you can answer my riddle."*

The man, whose name was Oedipus, trembled. If he could not answer the riddle, he would be torn apart and eaten. But he knew he had no choice.

"What is your riddle?"

The monster's smile was cruel.

"What is it that walks first on four legs, then on two legs, and finally on three legs?"

Oedipus thought for a long while. The Sphinx began to circle about him. It moved closer and closer, ready to pounce.

Nobody knew the answer to its riddle—nobody.

Finally, Oedipus replied.

"The answer is 'man.' He crawls on all fours as a baby, then learns to walk on two legs, and finally needs a cane in his old age."

The furious Sphinx *howled* with rage. Oedipus had answered the riddle correctly!

The howls grew louder and louder.

Then, with a last, terrible **SCREAM**, the monster flung itself off the mountain to its death on the rocks below.

Read a riddle

Long ago, people took riddles very seriously. The riddle of the Sphinx is one of the oldest and best-known riddles of all. Like all riddles, it's a puzzle with a hidden meaning that must be thought out or guessed.

Today, most riddles are silly questions with silly answers. They're called conundrums. What's a conundrum? It's a riddle based on an imaginary likeness between things that are as different as chalk is from cheese.

The answer to a conundrum is a play on words that usually makes people laugh —or at least smile or grin. See how often you laugh, smile, or grin when you learn the answers to these conundrums:

What tree:
1. has many friends? (poplar)
2. sighs a lot?
3. cries a lot?
4. is a couple?
5. does everyone carry in their hands?

What flower is:
1. a dairy product and a dish?
2. a country with many cars?
3. a cow's mistake?
4. watched over by shepherds?
5. what he did when he sat on a tack?

What letter of the alphabet is:

1. an insect that makes money for people who sell honey?
2. where "The Owl and the Pussycat" went to?
3. in your head?
4. a bird that chatters?
5. a small, round, green vegetable?

What two letters of the alphabet form a:

1. number between 75 and 85?
2. word that means "to rot"?
3. word that means "simple"?
4. word that means "frozen"?
5. word that means "an Indian tent"?

What part of your body is:

1. part of a clock?
2. a tropical tree?
3. a cut of meat?
4. bent macaroni?
5. a student?
6. a flower?
7. a pot cover?
8. corn on the cob?
9. first part of a rocket?
10. part of a river?
11. a bed of spring flowers?
12. part of a shoe?
13. the edge of a saw?
14. a young cow?

Answers: (tree) 1. poplar 2. pine 3. weeping willow 4. pear 5. palm (flower) 1. buttercup 2. carnation 3. cowslip 4. phlox 5. rose (one letter) 1. B 2. C 3. I 4. J 5. P (two letters) 1. A-T 2. D-K 3. E-Z 4. I-C 5. T-P (body) 1. hands 2. palm 3. shoulder 4. elbow 5. pupil 6. iris 7. lid 8. ear 9. nose 10. mouth 11. two lips—tulips 12. tongue 13. teeth 14. calf

Read a riddle
(continued)

What:

1. is the longest word in the English language?
2. part of a new watch has been used before?
3. animal changes size twice a day?
4. has eighteen legs and catches flies?
5. makes the Tower of Pisa lean?
6. is the quickest way for a man with a live goose on top of a high building to get down?
7. grows larger the more you take from it?
8. was the highest mountain before Mount Everest was discovered?
9. is the difference between a hill and a pill?
10. is the difference between a jeweler and a jailer?

When:

1. does a doctor get mad?
2. is a spotted dog likely to enter a house?
3. is it all right to serve milk in a saucer?
4. will water stop running downhill?

Why:

1. is the heart of a tree like a dog's tail?
2. isn't your nose twelve inches long?
3. was the wheel the greatest of all inventions?
4. didn't the three giants walking under one small umbrella get wet?
5. is the letter U the happiest in the alphabet?

If:

1. two is company and three's a crowd, what are four and five?

Answers: (what) 1. Smiles, because there's a mile between the first and last letters. 2. The second hand. 3. A cat, because you let it out at night and take it in every morning. 4. A baseball team. 5. It never eats. 6. By plucking the goose. 7. A hole. 8. Mount Everest. 9. A hill is hard to get up and a pill is hard to get down. 10. One sells watches, the other watches cells. (when) 1. When he's out of patients. 2. When the door is open. 3. To feed the cat. 4. When it gets to the bottom. (why) 1. Because it's farthest from the bark. 2. Because then it would be a foot. 3. Because it really started things rolling. 4. Because it wasn't raining. 5. Because it's in the middle of *fun*. (if) 1. Nine.

Just for p(h)un

Snow White has a father named Egg—Egg White. Get the yolk?

That is a pun, and puns are another way to have fun with language.

What's a pun? It's a funny way of saying something while meaning something else. You "play" with words.

Pun words sound alike, but are usually spelled differently. And they mean different things.

For example, an *ant* is never a relative, and an *aunt* is never an insect.

A baker can bake bread without *flower*, and a florist can make a bouquet without *flour*.

But a barber, who cuts *hair*, never gives a rabbit a *hare* cut.

Words such as *ant* and *aunt*, *flower* and *flour*, *hair* and *hare*, are known as homonyms. A homonym describes two or more words that sound alike but mean different things. The words may or may not be spelled the same.

The word *homonym* comes from the Greek. It means "same name." And homonyms are a good source for puns.

Here are some homonyms used in puns:

Eight famous mathematicians ate dinner together, so the headline read, "Eight ate eight dinners at eight."	**eight–ate**
A poison berry can bury you unless, of course, it's really a boysenberry.	**berry–bury**
It can cost a lot of dough to shoot a doe out of season.	**dough–doe**
The ecologist bought his wife a fir for Christmas. He thought it was fur enough.	**fir–fur**
A horse is a horse, but a sick pony is a little hoarse.	**horse–hoarse**
A pair of trees may grow pears—unless the pair are pines.	**pair–pear**

See how many more puns you can find in the conundrums on pages 244-247.

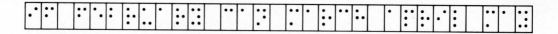

Braille is a code for blind people to read by touch. The dots above stand for letters of the alphabet. But instead of printed dots, the dots are raised in braille. Then it's possible to move one's fingertips along the raised dots and tell by touch what's written.

To find out what this pun says, check the braille alphabet on pages 186-209.

Running back again

"Otto, the pup," said Mom, "has lots of pep at noon!"

How many palindromes can you find in that sentence? The word *palindrome* comes from a Greek word and means "running back again." So, a palindrome is a word, a group of words, or a sentence that "runs back again" the same way it started. That's the fun of a palindrome. The first sentence has five palindromes: Otto, pup, Mom, pep, and noon.

Here are some famous palindromes. They make as much sense when you read them backward as they do when you read them forward:

MADAM, I'M ADAM.

NAME NO ONE MAN.

ABLE WAS I ERE I SAW ELBA.

A MAN, A PLAN, A CANAL—PANAMA!

P	E	P	H	E	Y	E	S	E	E
A	B	C	U	A	S	A	H	A	M
L	O	E	V	E	N	A	N	S	O
I	O	A	E	T	B	N	D	I	R
N	B	S	G	O	A	D	A	L	D
D	W	E	B	T	I	N	D	H	N
R	Y	E	F	T	O	O	T	A	I
O	F	S	M	O	M	O	O	N	L
M	P	U	P	P	Y	N	I	N	A
E	M	O	R	D	N	I	L	A	P

PEP
EYE
SEES
NOON
MOM
DAD
NAN
ADA
EVE
ASA
BOB
OTTO
AVA
ANNA
HANNAH
PUP
TOOT
BOOB

Directions: The list of one-word palindromes appears in the palindrome puzzle. They appear not only forward and backward, but also up, down, and diagonally. Copy the puzzle on a sheet of ruled paper. Then find and mark the palindromes, as shown. Two palindromes appear more than once. Can you find them?

Some people can't hear or speak. But they can spell words by making signs with their fingers.

To learn what this palindrome is, check the finger alphabet on pages 186–209.

Mr. Fister's Tongue Twister

Read this story aloud. You won't believe what happens.

Mr. Fister's sister Sue enjoys 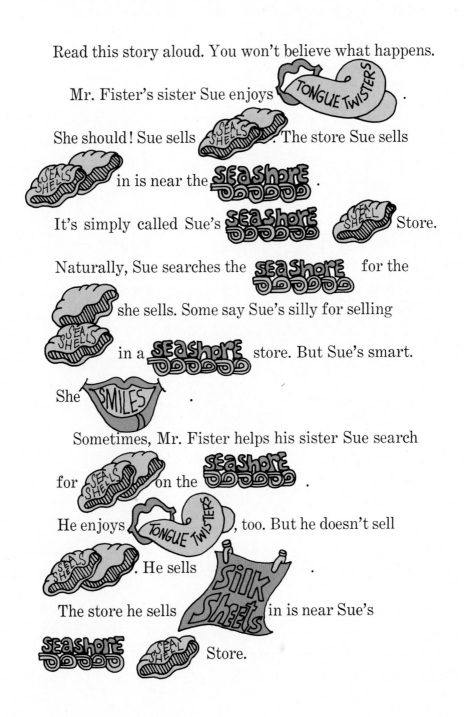 .

She should! Sue sells . The store Sue sells

in is near the .

It's simply called Sue's Store.

Naturally, Sue searches the for the

she sells. Some say Sue's silly for selling

in a store. But Sue's smart.

She .

Sometimes, Mr. Fister helps his sister Sue search

for on the .

He enjoys , too. But he doesn't sell

. He sells .

The store he sells in is near Sue's

Store.

It's called Mr. Fister's ⟨Seashore⟩ ⟨Silk Sheets⟩ Store.

One day, Mr. Fister told his sister Sue, "I sold six

⟨Silk Sheets⟩ ⟨Silk Sheets⟩ to six ⟨SHEIKS⟩ who came into my

⟨Seashore⟩ ⟨Silk Sheets⟩ Store!"

Mr. Fister's sister Sue ⟨SHRIEKED⟩. "Those

must be the same six ⟨SHEIKS⟩ I sold sixty

⟨SEA SHELLS⟩!"

"Shucks," said Mr. Fister, "the same six ⟨SHEIKS⟩

must have visited your ⟨Seashore⟩ ⟨SEA SHELL⟩

Store after buying six ⟨Silk Sheets⟩ in my store."

"Yesh," ⟨SMILED⟩ Sue.

Mr. Fister chuckled. "Selling **shix** silk **seets**

to the **shame** six sheiks

who bought **shixty she sells**

seems to have twisted your tongue, my dear **Shue**!"

And that was Mr. Fister's  ⟨TONGUE TWISTER⟩ .

More tongue twisters

Mr. Fister and his sister have more
tongue twisters to share. They suggest
you read them aloud, lickety-split.
(That's slang for "as fast as you can.")
The first is probably the best-known
tongue twister.

Peter Piper picked a peck of pickled peppers.
A peck of pickled peppers Peter Piper picked.
If Peter Piper picked a peck of pickled peppers,
Where is the peck of pickled peppers
Peter Piper picked?

The words *tooter* and *tutor* sound the
same. But they mean different things.
A tooter toots. A tutor teaches.

A tooter who tooted a flute,
tried to tutor two tutors to toot.
Said the two to the tutor,
"Is it harder to toot or
To tutor two tutors to toot?"
And the tutor said, "To toot!"

Short tongue twisters can tangle and trip your tongue, too. Try reading these aloud, quickly.

Thistle sifters sift thistles.

The bootblack brought the book back.

The sixth sheik's sixth sheep's sick.

Greek grape growers grow great Greek grapes.

Beth bought a big blue bucket of blue blueberries.

Sister Susie's sewing sheets for six sick soldiers.

Round and round the rugged rock the ragged rascal ran.

The International Flag Code uses different flags to stand for letters of the alphabet. The flags are used to spell out messages from one ship to another. The flags are run up, or hoisted, on a rope. Each ship has a codebook to help send messages in different languages.

The flags shown spell out a person's name. If you keep repeating the name as fast as you can, you'll see it's a flag-twisting tongue twister.

To find out what it is, check the International Flag Alphabet on pages 186–209.

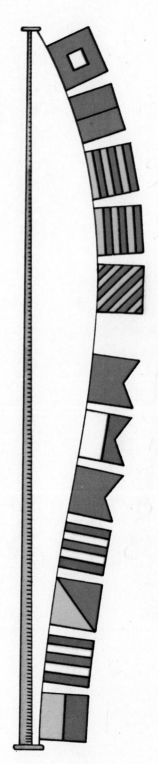

256

My grandmother likes tea,
but she doesn't like milk.

Word games

My Grandmother Likes Tea

The leader begins by saying, "My grandmother likes tea, but she doesn't like coffee." Then each player, in turn, says, "My grandmother likes tea," and names something that she doesn't like. The leader agrees—if a player uses a word without the letter T in it. This is the key to the whole game. Grandmother likes anything with the letter T in it.

For example, suppose a player says, "My grandmother likes tea, but she doesn't like toast." This would be wrong. The leader would say, "My grandmother

My grandmother likes tea,
but she doesn't like coffee.

My grandmother likes tea,
but she doesn't like toast.

likes toast, but she doesn't like bread."
But the leader doesn't tell the player
why. Each player has to figure this out
for himself. The game continues until
everyone gets the idea.

Our Cook Doesn't Like Peas

This game is played in much the same
way as My Grandmother Likes Tea. The
only difference is that only the leader
knows the cook doesn't like any food
with the letter P in it. For example, "Our
cook doesn't like peas, but likes
carrots." But you may not say, "Our
cook doesn't like peas, but likes peppers."
The word *pepper* is full of "p's."

My grandmother likes toast,
but she doesn't like bread.

Word games
(continued)

Calling All Cities!

The leader calls out the name of any big city. The next player must name another city before the leader can count to ten. The name of this city must start with the last letter in the name of the city just called. Otherwise, the player is out. The winner is the last remaining player.

Word Snap!

The leader needs two or more sets of alphabet cards. The leader calls out a category, such as animals, and holds up one of the alphabet cards.

The first player to call out an animal name that begins with the letter shown, gets the card. The winner is the player who ends up with the most cards.

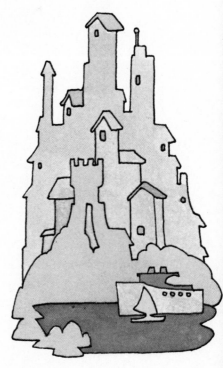

Word games
(continued)

Grocery Store

The Grocer stands before two teams, each lined up in single file. A player from each team steps up to the Grocer. The Grocer calls out a letter of the alphabet. The first player to call out the name of a grocery item that starts with the letter the Grocer called scores a point. The team with the most points wins the game.

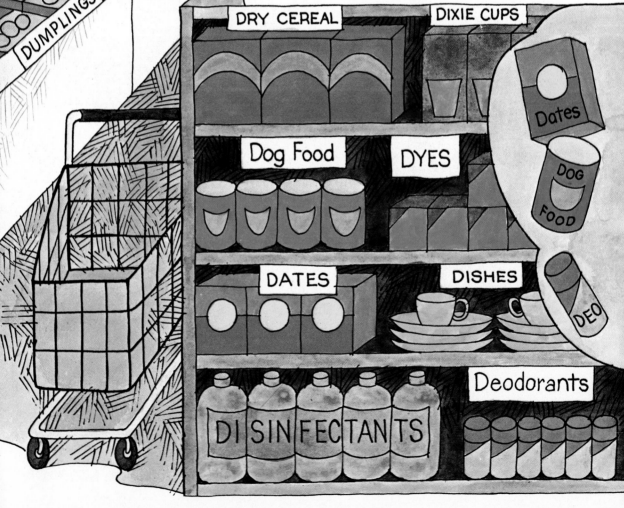

Word Hunt

Although harder, this game is much like Grocery Store. Instead of just calling out a letter of the alphabet, the leader also calls a category. For example, "Games—B"; "Insects—M"; "Countries —A." The reply to "Games—B" could be baseball; to "Insects—M" it might be mosquito; and to "Countries—A" it could be Australia. The first player who answers scores a point for his team. The team with the most points is the winner.

Word games
(continued)

A Was An Apple Pie

This game tells what happens to an apple pie. The first player says, "A Was An Apple Pie. A ate it." The other players, in turn, tell what might have happened to the pie. Each player must think of an action word that starts with the next letter of the alphabet. Anyone who can't, must drop out of the game. The last player left is the winner.

Teapot

The leader thinks of a word. Each player, in turn, asks a question to help find out what the word is.

To do this, the players substitute the word *teapot* for the unknown word. The leader may answer only "Yes" or "No" to the questions. For example, if the unknown word is *run*, and a player asks, "Do I teapot with my legs?" the leader says, "Yes." But the answer to "Does the sun teapot?" is "No."

The first player to guess the word is the next leader.

enter
PIeS
heRe
For
PiE
CONTEST

I love my love with an A because he is angelic.

I love my love with a B because she is brave.

I Love My Love

I love my love with an A because she is **a**dorable.
I love my love with a B because he is **b**right.

And so the game goes, through the alphabet. Each player takes the next letter to describe why "I love my love." If a player can't think of a word before the leader counts to ten, the player is out.

The Minister's Cat

This game is played in much the same way as I Love My Love. The key sentence is "The minister's cat is a(n) _____ cat." Each player describes the cat, using a word that begins with the letter A. If a player misses, or repeats a word that's been used, he has a point scored against him. After each player has had a turn, the cat is described using a word that begins with

I love my love with a C because he is clumsy.

I love my love with a D because she is devilish.

the letter B, and so on through the alphabet. The player with the most points loses!

Dumb Crambo

Team 1 leaves the room. Team 2 remains and agrees on a word that describes an action, such as run, skip, or bounce. Team 1 must guess and act out this word.

When Team 1 returns, the only clue Team 2 gives is a word that rhymes with the word they chose.

Team 1 agrees on a word they think the action word might be. From that point on, no one must speak.

Team 1 acts out the word they guessed. If they're wrong, the members of Team 2 shake their heads. Then Team 1 must agree on another word they think the action word might be. When Team 1 guesses and acts out the right word, Team 2 claps. Team 2 then leaves the room and Team 1 thinks of an action word.

266

"Where are you going?"
"To Donegal."

"What will you do there?"
"Dunk doughnuts."

Word games
(continued)

Where Are You Going?

Each player tells the leader where he or she is going and what they will do there. The players must answer quickly. And they must say what they will do in two words. Both words must begin with the same letter as the place the player is going to. Otherwise, the player is out. Each player must pick a new place to go to and a new thing to do.

Snip!

"It" stands inside a circle of players and tosses a knotted handkerchief to any player. At the same time, "It" calls out a three-letter word, spells the word, counts to twelve, and says, "Snip!"

The player who catches the handkerchief must say three words that begin with the letters in the word.

Let's say "It" calls, "Dog, d-o-g." The player with the handkerchief might yell, "Doctor, Oats, Ginger." If he does this before "It" counts to twelve and says "Snip!" he's safe.

But if "It" counts to twelve and says "Snip!" first, the player is out, o-u-t.

The last one out is the winner.

Birds, Beasts, Fishes, or Flowers

Two teams line up opposite each other, with a good running distance between them.

Team 1 picks one of the categories in the title, and an example, such as: Bird—cardinal. This team then crosses to face Team 2. They shout out the category —in this example—"Bird" and the first letter of the bird they chose—"C."

When Team 2 guesses "cardinal," the players on Team 1 run for their side.

Team 2 chases them. Any player tagged before reaching his side must join Team 2.

Then Team 2 gets a turn. The team that loses the most players loses the game.

Word games
(continued)

Action Spelling Bee

Have you ever wondered why we call a spelling contest a spelling bee? A bee is a social gathering, where people work and talk. It got this name because such gatherings are like busy honeybees working together to make honey.

In a spelling bee, the leader makes a list of words. Then, two teams see which can correctly spell the most words.

If a player misspells a word, a member of the other team gets a chance to spell the same word. Guess what happens if a player misspells a word. You're right. He's out.

The rules for Action Spelling Bee are the same, except for one thing. Hand signs are used for the vowels (a, e, i, o, and u), as shown. Any player who uses the wrong sign, or says a vowel, is out. The winner is the last player remaining.

Secret Word

The pictures show you how this game is played. What word would you use to describe what is happening in each picture? The clown is *somersaulting, leaping, opening,* and *walking.* Put the first letters of the words together and you have the secret word, which is *slow.*

Form equal groups. Each group agrees on a secret word. The secret word must have as many letters as there are players in the group.

One after another, the players act out words that begin with letters that, when put together, spell the secret word.

The other groups try to guess the words being acted out. The group that guesses the secret word gets to do their word.

Fruit Basket Upset

Each player picks and calls out the name of a fruit. The players form a large circle, with "It" in the middle.

"It" calls out the names of any two fruits. For example, if "apple and orange" is called, the players who chose apple and orange must change places at once. If "It" beats either player to his place, that player is "It."

To really get some action going, "It" may shout "Fruit Basket Upset!" Then all players must change places.

Word games
(continued)

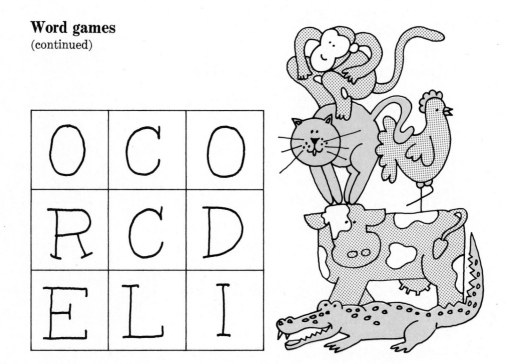

Puzzle Box

An animal is hiding in these boxes. What is it? To
find out, read on. After you learn how to make your
own Puzzle Box, you'll be able to figure out the
answer. And then you can make other puzzles and
test your friends.

Draw a square with nine boxes. Think of a
nine-letter word—any nine-letter word—and print
the letters in the boxes. The letters must follow each
other, like the cars of a train. You can go in any
direction, but you must not skip a square.

In the puzzle shown, the first letter of the animal's
name is in the center square. The second letter is to
the left of the first letter. And the last letter is
in the lower left-hand square. Now can you work it?

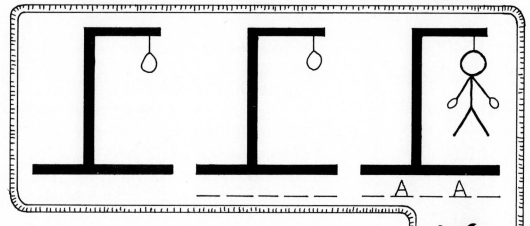

Hangman

This is a fun word game for two players. The first player to be the hangman draws a gallows and a rope. He or she thinks of a five-letter word and puts five dashes under the gallows. The hangman also prints the letters of the alphabet, as shown.

The other player tries to guess the hangman's word by calling out one letter at a time. When a letter is called, the hangman crosses it off the alphabet. If the letter is in the word, the hangman fills in the exact dash. If a letter appears more than once, it is put in each place where it appears.

If the player picks a letter that's not in the word, the hanging starts. The hanging is done in this order:

1. head
2. body
3. left arm
4. right arm
5. left hand
6. right hand
7. left leg
8. right leg
9. left foot
10. right foot

This gives the player ten chances to guess the word. If the player is hung, he loses the game and must try to guess another word. But if he guesses the word before he is hung, he gets to be the hangman.

Word games
(continued)

Scrambled Names

Here are three sets of scrambled names. Get a pencil and paper and copy the words. See how long it takes you to unscramble them.

The scrambled days and months should be easy. But the scrambled cities are harder. Some of the cities may stump you. If you have a problem unscrambling the cities, you'll find the answers at the bottom of the first page of this book.

Scrambled Days

STUDYEA   AFRDYI
RUTHYADS   YNMODA
TUAARYDS   DEEDSWAYN
AYSNUD

RAYBEUFR

YARNJUA

HARCM

Scrambled Months

PLAIR	ROVMEBEN
RAYBEUFR	ROOTBEC
HARCM	ATSUGU
REEDBECM	PEERSMETB
YARNJUA	AYM
ENJU	LUYJ

Scrambled Cities

ICHOGCA	RUNFAFKTR
NODLNO	YESNDY
RASPI	YOOTK
MORE	ROOTNOT

You can have fun scrambling words for
other players to unscramble. Scramble
the names of states and provinces.
Just be sure you don't leave out
any letters when you scramble a word.

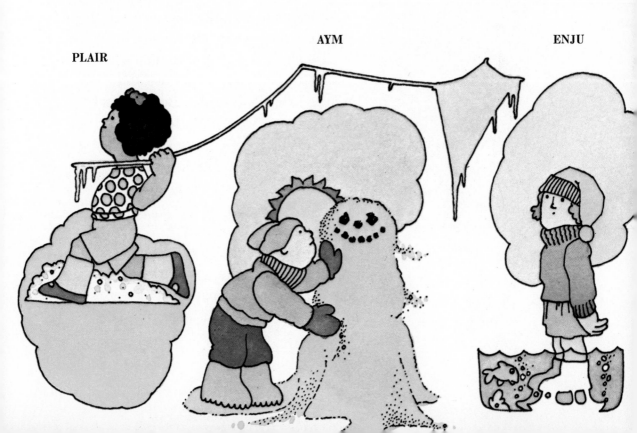

PLAIR   AYM   ENJU

Word games
(continued)

Squeeze

If letters could be stuffed into a tube, how many different words could you squeeze from a tube filled with "Twinkle, Twinkle, Little Star"?

You may use only the letters in the title. And in any one word you may not use a letter more often that it appears in "Twinkle, Twinkle, Little Star."

For example, you may not use words that have more than one *a*, *r*, or *s*, because there is only one of each of these letters. So, you could use *ark*, because it has only one *a*. But *aardvark* would be very wrong. Not only does it have three *a*'s and two *r*'s, it also has *d* and *v*, letters you may not use. You may use as many as five *t*'s, four *l*'s, three *e*'s and *i*'s, and two *k*'s, *n*'s, and *w*'s in any one word.

You can play this game alone or in a group. If played in a group, the player who makes up the longest list of words in a given time is the winner.

Word / Category	S	M	I	L	E
Animal					
City					
Flower					
Food					
Famous People					

Categories

To play this game, make copies of the form shown, one for each player.

The players write in names for each category. Each name must start with the letter shown at the top of the column.

For example, when the animal category is complete, it might read *squirrel, monkey, impala, lion,* and *elephant.*

Players have up to ten minutes to fill in the form. The winner is the first one to fill in the boxes correctly.

You can change the game by using different categories and a different word at the top.

Word games
(continued)

SCOUT	SLIDE	CRAWL
SHARE	GLOW	GREAT
CHILD	FLOWER	FRIEND
GHOST	SMALL	TREAT
SKY	SNOW	PRINT
BLACK	SPELL	STAR
CLEAR	BROOK	TWIN
PLAY	DRAW	SWING

Spell-O!

To play this game you need to do some work first, but the excitement makes the game worth the work.

First, print each of the above words on a slip of paper. Fold the slips and put them into a big bowl. Now, make a card, like the one shown, for each player. Be sure to mark an X in the middle box.

Give each player a card and pencil and you're all set to start Spell-O! Tell the players you're going to call out some words. As each word is called, they are to write the first two letters of the word in any one box. For example, if the first word is *scout*, they mark *sc* in any one box.

Pick slips and call out words until all the players have filled each box. Fold the slips and put them back in the container.

Now the exciting part of the game begins. Pull a slip, read the word aloud, and set the slip aside. The players mark an X through the box with the first two letters of the word you called. Do this until one or more players cross out a row down, across, or on a diagonal, or have crossed out the four corners of the card. The first to do this shouts, "Spell-O!"

Double-check the crossed-out row against the slips set aside. The winner leaves the game. Continue as before until there's another winner. Each time, the winner drops out. When all words have been called, the game is over. If prizes are offered, winners choose in the order they won.

Word games
(continued)

Anagrams

You can play Anagrams with up to eight players. It's well worth the time it takes to make a set of two hundred letters to play this game. The letters can be used over and over again.

Cut out two hundred 1-inch (2.5-cm) squares from construction paper or light cardboard. Print a letter on one side of each square. You will need:

fourteen each of A, E, I, O
ten of S
nine each of B, C, D, F, G, H, L, M, N, R, T
five of U
four each of K, P, V, W, Y, J
two each of Q, X, Z

Here's how you play Anagrams. Scatter the letters facedown on a table. Clear a space in the center where players place the letters they turn up.

john huehnergarth

The first player turns up one letter. Let's say the letter is *U*. The next play is to the left. This player turns up the letter *S*. *US* is a word, so the second player takes the *U* and puts the word at his place.

Player number three turns up the letter *E*. Aha! By adding the letter *E* to *US* he can make the word *USE*. So he takes the word *US* and makes the word *USE* at his place. He's stolen the word from another player—and that's how the game is played.

The fourth player can't do anything with the letter *G* he turns up. So he passes to the fifth player. Suppose this player turns up the letter *T*. He can use any turned-up letter or complete word to form a new word. He has one minute to think of a possible word and comes up with *GUEST*. He places the word before him. Then it's the next player's turn, and so it goes.

Players can try to protect their words by adding new letters when it's their turn. The first player with five words wins the game. Then you can start all over again. Use a dictionary to check any challenged words.

Secret messages

You and your friends can have lots of fun sending secret messages. Use invisible writing, codes, or ciphers! If you exchange messages in one of these three ways, no one else will be able to find out your secrets.

Invisible writing, of course, is writing that you can't see unless you know how to make it appear.

Codes and ciphers are two kinds of secret messages. Most people think that codes and ciphers are the same. But they're not.

A code uses a secret word, number, or sign to stand for a whole word, a complete sentence, or even a whole message.

A cipher uses a secret letter, number, or sign for every letter in a message.

To prepare a secret message, you have to encode or encipher it. Then, to read the secret message, you have to decode or decipher it.

Read on to find out how you can write and read secret messages just the way kings, generals, pirates, and spies have done for thousands of years.

Invisible Writing

You can send a mystery message on a sheet of paper that looks blank! The trick is using what's known as invisible ink. This special ink isn't really invisible. But when it dries, you can't see it.

Lemon juice makes a good invisible ink. Just squeeze some lemon juice into a small dish or glass. Write your message with an ordinary penpoint or a wooden toothpick. Be sure the invisible ink is dry before you send off your message.

The message will mysteriously appear when the paper is heated. Hold the paper over a lighted electric bulb. In less than a minute the writing will start to appear. Move the paper around until you can read all the words.

Secret messages
(continued)

Secret Codes

Codes are a good way to send and receive secret messages. But there is one problem. You have to have a codebook. You need so many code words, numbers, or signs that you could never remember them all.

Spies who worked for George Washington during the American Revolution had a simple number code. You can make one like it very easily. All you need is a dictionary. Washington's spies just copied out of a dictionary all the words they might need. Each word was given a number. It was a simple system because the words were numbered in alphabetical order. For example: troops 635; war 680; was 681, and so on. There were also numbers for the names of people and places. George Washington was 711 and New York City was 727.

Another kind of code is the International Flag Code. But this isn't a secret code. Navies of many countries use the International Flag Code. The code has flags and pennants that stand for letters, numbers, and complete messages. You can see the International Flag Alphabet on pages 186–209.

Alphabet Ciphers

YVDZIV   LU   GSV   NLMHGVI

Martian talk? Gibberish? A foreign language? Not at all! It's a simple alphabet cipher. Here's the key:

Z Y X W V U T S R Q P O N M L K J I H G F E D C B A
A B C D E F G H I J K L M N O P Q R S T U V W X Y Z

As you can see, in this cipher the letters are in reverse order, with Z first and A last. To decipher the message, look for Y on the top line. The letter below Y is B. So, Y stands for B; V stands for E; D stands for W; Z for A; and I stands for R. Run the letters together and they spell BEWARE, the first word of the secret message. What does the message tell you to beware of?

For another kind of alphabet cipher, all you need to write or read a message is a copy of the alphabet. When you encipher a message, use the letter to the right of the real letter. Thus A becomes B, and so on. And Z, of course, becomes A. When you want to decipher the message, use the letter to the left of the message letter. Thus B stands for A and A for Z.

The famous Roman general Julius Caesar used a cipher like this more than two thousand years ago. In his cipher, he used the letter three places to the right of the real letter. Using his system, you would encipher the word ATTACK as DWWDFN.

You can make other ciphers by reversing this system and using letters to the left of the real letters.

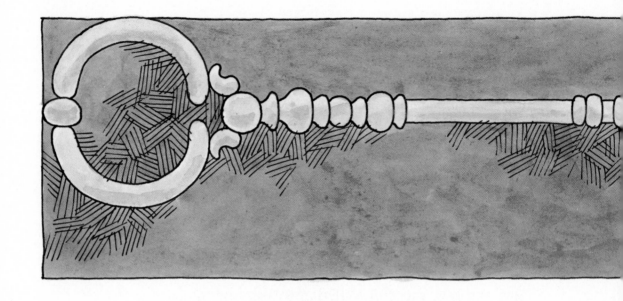

Secret messages
(continued)

Number Ciphers

13 5 5 20 13 5 1 20 20 8 5
4 5 1 4 15 1 11 20 18 5 5

This jumble of numbers is really a secret message, or cipher. Here's how to find out what it says.

Each number stands for a letter of the alphabet:

1	2	3	4	5	6	7	8	9	10	11	12	13
A	B	C	D	E	F	G	H	I	J	K	L	M

14	15	16	17	18	19	20	21	22	23	24	25	26
N	O	P	Q	R	S	T	U	V	W	X	Y	Z

Now that you have the key, the rest is easy. For example, 13 stands for M; 5 stands for E; 20 stands for T. So the first secret word is MEET. You're on your own to figure out the rest of the secret message.

You can use this cipher and others to send secret messages to your friends. But be sure to make them a copy of the key so they can decipher the messages.

For another cipher that uses numbers, you can make A number 26 and Z number 1:

26	25	24	23	22	21	20	19	18	17
A	B	C	D	E	F	G	H	I	J and so on.

You can also skip numbers in a pattern. For example, give every other letter an even and an odd number:

2	1	4	3	6	5	8	7	10	9
A	B	C	D	E	F	G	H	I	J and so on.

Or, you can give a letter any number you want:

10	21	37	42	57	63	78	89	94	101
A	B	C	D	E	F	G	H	I	J and so on.

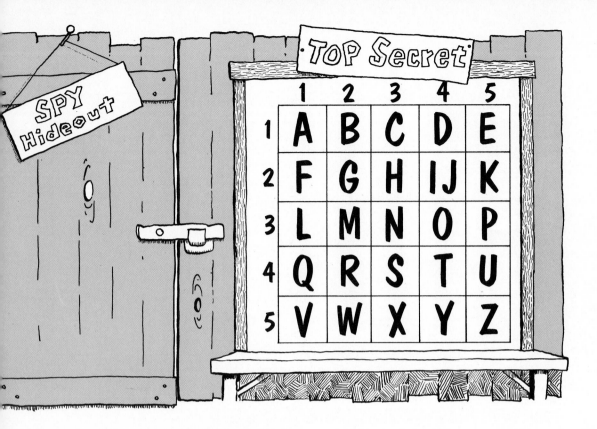

Secret messages
(continued)

Box Cipher

43 23 24 35   11 23 34 54 !

Each number in this cipher has two digits. The first digit tells you which line the letter appears on. The second digit tells you which column it is in.

For example, 43 means you'll find the letter on line 4, where it meets column 3. So 43 stands for S. Note that 24 stands for either I or J. But you won't have any trouble figuring out which letter 24 stands for once you see the whole word.

You can use the cipher box to make up your own secret messages. Just be sure to give a copy of the cipher box to the person with whom you want to share secret messages. Then your friend can decipher your messages and send you secret messages, too.

Pigpen Cipher

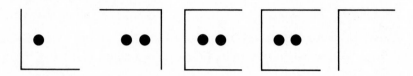

Here's the key to this secret message:

A B C	D E F	G H I
J K L	M N O	P Q R
S T U	V W X	Y Z

Each letter of the secret message is shown by the shape of the pigpen and the number of dots. Look at the shape of the first pigpen in the secret message. It is the same shape as the top right-hand pigpen in the key. But each pigpen has a group of letters. How do you know which is the right letter?

It's simple. If the pigpen has no dot, it means the first letter in the pen. If the pigpen has one dot, it means the second letter in the pen. And if the pigpen has two dots, it means the third letter in the pen.

In this case, there is one dot in the first pigpen. One dot means the second letter. Look at the top right-hand pigpen in the key. The second letter is H. So H is the first letter in the message.

Now that you know how it works, can you decipher the rest of the secret message?

Secret messages
(continued)

The Mysterious Message

The following message appears in a famous short story, "The Gold-Bug," by Edgar Allan Poe. It looks like a jumble of type, but it's really a cipher that tells where a pirate treasure is buried.

53‡‡†305))6*;4826)4‡.)4‡);806*;48†8¶60))85;1‡(;:‡*8†
83(88)5*†;46(;88*96*?;8)*‡(;485);5*†2:*‡(;4956*2(5*—
4)8¶8*;4069285);)6†8)4‡‡;1(‡9;48081;8:8‡1;48†85;4)485†
528806*81(‡9;48;(88;4(‡?34;48)4‡;161;:188;‡?;

How was the message deciphered? First, the hero made a list of the different symbols and counted the number of times each appeared. The number 8 was used most often. Now, in English, the letter *e* is used more often than any other letter. So *e* was substituted for every 8.

To test this idea, two checks were made. Many English words, such as *meet* and *been*, have two *e*'s together. The hero found that in the cipher there were five places where *e* was doubled. Now, of all the short words in English, *the* is used most often. So, he looked to see how often 8 was used after two other symbols that were always the same. He found that the symbols ;48 appeared together seven times. If ;48 stood for *the*, then each ; stood for *t*, each 4 for *h*, and each 8 for *e*. Working this way, he finally deciphered the message. Here's what it said:

> A good glass in the Bishop's hostel in the
> Devil's seat forty-one degrees and thirteen
> minutes northeast and by north main branch
> seventh limb east side shoot from the left
> eye of the death's head a bee line from the
> tree through the shot fifty feet out.

This mysterious message led the hero to a spooky place where he found a buried treasure of gold and gems. If you read the story, you'll find out just how he worked out the meaning of the message.

Secret Languages

If you can read the print on the little pig's shirt, you know pig Latin. But if you don't know this popular secret language, it's easy to learn. Then you and your friends can talk to each other without some other people knowing what you're saying!

For most words in pig Latin, all you do is place the first letter of a word at the end of the word and add ay. For example, you say "ecretsay anguagelay" for "secret language." For short words like *and, if,* and *the,* just add ay to the end of the word.

And if the first two letters of a word make one sound when spoken, switch both letters of the word to the end and add ay. The word *when* becomes *enwhay, this* becomes *isthay,* and so on.

Another secret language is known as Na. It's even easier to speak than pig Latin. All you do is add na after every word. Here's the first line of "Jack and Jill" in Na language.

Jackna andna Jillna wentna upna ana hillna.

A third secret language is called Gree. It's like Na, except that you add gree after each spoken word:

Jackgree andgree Jillgree wentgree. . . .

Now that you've learned how to speak three secret languages, what would happen if you mixed them all together? You'd get something like this:

Isthay isna thegree endna ofay unfay withna wordsgree. Gogree ackbay andna artstay againgree!

Books to Read

There are many exciting and interesting children's books about language, writing, and the history of words. Some of the books listed here tell the true stories of how we have learned about languages and writing. Others are storybooks in which language plays a part. And some are filled with tongue twisters, puzzles, and secret codes. Look for these books, and others like them, in your school or public library. And happy reading!

All Ages

Fun with Puzzles, by Joseph Leeming (1946, Lippincott)
Puzzles of every kind for everybody. This book has brain twisters, anagrams, and word puzzles for readers to solve. And the answers are in the back of the book.

Handtalk: An ABC of Finger Spelling and Sign Language,
    by Remy Charlip, Mary Beth Miller, and George Ancona
    (1974, Parents' Magazine Press)
You can talk with your eyes, your face, your hands, and your body. This book shows the signs used for letters and words. At the bottom of each page, there is a mystery word for readers to solve.

Ages 3 to 5

Listed below are a few of the many fine alphabet books for young children. These books show each letter and usually give words in which the sounds are used. The attractive, fanciful illustrations and fun-to-say words capture and hold the attention of young and old alike.

ABC, by Bruno Munari (1960, World)

ABC, by Dr. Seuss (1963, Random House)

ABC of Things, by Helen Oxenbury (1972, Watts)

The Alphabet Boat—A Seagoing Alphabet Book, by George
    Mendoza (1972, American Heritage)

The Alphabet Tale, by Jan Garten (1964, Random House)

The Alphabet Tree, by Leo Lionni (1968, Pantheon)

Hosie's Alphabet, by Leonard Baskin (1972, Viking)

Ages 5 to 8

A & The, by Ellen Raskin (1970, Atheneum)
A book for everyone who can read the words *a* and *the*. It's a mystery, too. What do William T. C. Baumgarten's middle initials stand for?

A Gaggle of Geese, by Eve Merriam (1960, Knopf)
A group of elephants is called a herd. But what do you call a group of turkeys? You can find out in this book.

ABC's of the Earth, by Isaac Asimov (1971, Walker)
Avalanches, earthquakes, caves, glaciers, valleys, and volcanoes—the author defines two earth terms for each letter of the alphabet.

At Home: A Visit in Four Languages (1968, Macmillan)
In the Park: An Excursion in Four Languages (1968, Macmillan)
In School: Learning in Four Languages (1969, Macmillan)
A series of language books by Esther Hautzig. These books are a colorful introduction to familiar words in English, Spanish, French, and Russian.

Best Word Book Ever, by Richard Scarry (1973, Golden)
Bears, rabbits, cats, and other animals introduce words to beginning readers. Colorful pictures illustrate words from the farm, zoo, and other places.

Homographic Homophones (1973, Lerner)
More Antonyms (1973, Lerner)
More Homonyms (1973, Lerner)
More Synonyms (1973, Lerner)
Joan Hanson has written and illustrated this series of books about words and their sounds and meanings.

The Secret Language, by Ursula Nordstrom (1960, Harper)
Shy Victoria hates boarding school and is homesick until she makes a new friend, Martha. Martha speaks a secret language and teaches it to Victoria.

Sparkle and Spin, by Ann and Paul Rand (1957, Harcourt, Brace)
What is a word? How do we use words to communicate ideas? This colorful book answers these questions and more.

Words Inside Words, by Michael Sage (1961, Lippincott)
What word is in the word *box?* That's what this book is all about—words found within other words.

(continued on page 292)

Ages 9 to 12

A Twister of Twists, A Tangler of Tongues,
   by Alvin Schwartz (1972, Lippincott)
Try saying "cheap ship trips" or "rubber baby buggy
bumpers." These tongue twisters, plus many others, make
this book a challenge to read aloud.

Alvin's Secret Code, by Clifford Hicks
   (1963, Holt, Rinehart and Winston)
A book of mystery and adventure. Alvin, the Magnificent
Brain, deciphers a secret message and finds a lost treasure.

Danger—Men Talking!, by Stuart Chase
   (1969, Parents' Magazine Press)
An advanced book about animal and human speech development.
It also tells of some problems in human communication.

The First Book of Language, by Mauree Applegate (1962, Watts)
An introduction to grammar. The author shows the reader
the correct way to construct and punctuate a sentence.

Hieroglyphs for Fun: Your Own Secret Code Language,
   by Joseph and Lenore Scott (1974, Van Nostrand Reinhold)
This is a book about the mystery and romance of ancient
Egypt and Egyptian writing. The meanings of many hieroglyphs
are explained, and there are puzzles to be solved.

Man Must Speak, by Roy Gallant (1969, Random House)
The story of communication from animals and humans to
radio and television.

The Phantom Tollbooth, by Norton Juster (1961, Random House)
Milo takes a fantastic journey through the Phantom Tollbooth.
He discovers such strange places as Dictionopolis and the
Mountain of Ignorance.

Reading the Past, by Leonard Cottrell (1971, Macmillan)
This book for advanced readers gives a detailed
account of how Egyptian hieroglyphics, Babylonian cuneiform,
and other ancient written languages were deciphered.

The Romance of Writing, by Keith Gordon Irwin (1956, Viking)
This book takes advanced readers through the history of
writing, with stories about numbers and signs.

The Russian Alphabet Book, by Dr. Fan Parker
   (1961, Coward-McCann)
A book for readers who want to learn how to say Russian
letters and words. There is also historical and geographical
information about Russia.

Seeing Fingers: The Story of Louis Braille,
   by Etta DeGering (1962, David McKay)
A good biography of Louis Braille who, as a blind
fifteen-year-old, invented a system of writing that has made
it possible for the blind to read by touch.

The Stone That Spoke, by Steven Frimmer (1969, Putnam)
Language detectives follow many clues to try to learn how
to read ancient languages. This advanced book is about
their work and their contributions to archaeology.

The Tree of Language, by Helene and Charlton Laird (1957, World)
This history of the English language and the development
of writing includes many word stories, odd things about
words, and how to trace the history of words.

The 26 Letters, by Oscar Ogg (1961, Crowell)
A book about the history of writing and printing, with
many fine examples of different styles of lettering.

What a Funny Thing to Say!, by Bernice Kohn (1974, Dial)
How did the diaper and the Frisbee get their names? You
can find out in this book—along with information about
other words, slang terms, and secret codes.

Wonders in Words, by Maxwell Nurnberg (1968, Prentice-Hall)
Look closely—you will find that many of our words come from
superstitions, from place names, or from the names of animals.

Words Words Words, by Mary O'Neill (1966, Doubleday)
"Dash is a sign that writers make/Whenever their thoughts
switch or break." There are verses in this book about the
alphabet, the English language, and many other things.

Would you put your money in a sand bank?,
   by Harold Longman (1968, Rand McNally)
A book of homonyms. The author has written riddles, silly
questions, and poems made from words that look or sound
alike but have different meanings.

New Words

Here are some of the words you have met in this book. Some of these words you'll know, but most of them may be new to you. Since you'll see them again, they're good words to know. Many of the words have to do with language and writing, but others are just hard to pronounce. Next to each word you will see how to say the word: **accent** (AK sehnt). The part shown in capital letters is said a little more loudly than the rest of the word. Under each word are one or two sentences that tell you what the word means.

abbreviation (uh bree vee AY shuhn)

An abbreviation is a shortened form of a word or phrase. For example, the abbreviation for minute is min. and P.O. stands for post office.

Aborigine (ab uh RIHJ uh nee)

The Aborigines are people whose ancestors were the first to live in Australia, long ago.

accent (AK sehnt)

An accent is the special way in which people of a particular group or place say, or pronounce, words.

addled (AD uhld)

Someone who is addled is confused or mixed up.

Algonkian (al GAHNG kee uhn)

Algonkian is a name for the languages of several tribes of American Indians.

anagram (AN uh gram)

An anagram is a word formed by rearranging the letters in a word so as to make another word. For example, *pot—top; north—thorn.*

ancestor (AN sehs tuhr)

An ancestor is one from whom a living thing is descended.

ancient (AYN shuhnt)

Anything that belongs to times long past is ancient.

Assyrian (uh SIHR ee uhn)

The Assyrians were people of an ancient country in the Middle East.

awesome (AW suhm)

An awesome sight is one that causes fear and wonder.

azure (AZH uhr)

Azure is the color of a clear-blue sky.

Babylonian (bab uh LOH nee uhn)

The Babylonians were people of an ancient country in the Middle East.

cannibal (KAN uh buhl)

A cannibal is a person who eats human flesh.

catapult (KAT uh puhlt)

A catapult was an ancient weapon that shot stones or arrows.

category (KAT uh gawr ee)

A category is a class or group, the members of which have something in common.

Celt (sehlt or kehlt)

The Celts were an ancient people of western Europe and the British Isles.

cipher (SY fuhr)

A cipher is secret writing that has a letter or symbol in place of each letter in the original message.

clod (klahd)

A clod is a dull and stupid person.

consonant (KON suh nuhnt)
A consonant is a letter or speech sound formed by changing or stopping the breath with the tongue, teeth, or lips. Letters such as *d*, *k*, *p*, and *t* are consonants.

conundrum (kuh NUHN druhm)
A conundrum is a riddle whose answer involves a pun or a play on words.

cuneiform (kyoo NEE uh fawrm)
Cuneiform is a kind of wedge-shaped writing which was invented by ancient people in the Middle East.

cursive script (KUHR sihv skrihpt)
Cursive script is handwriting that has flowing strokes and joined letters.

decipher (dee SY fuhr)
To decipher is to decode or figure out the meaning of a secret message.

devour (dih VOWR)
To devour is to eat like an animal.

dialect (DY uh lehkt)
A dialect is the way in which the people of a particular area speak and the words they use.

dictionary (DIHK shuh nehr ee)
A dictionary is a book that gives meanings, pronunciations, and other information about words.

din (dihn)
A din is a loud noise that seems to go on and on.

elegant (EHL uh guhnt)
Anything elegant is beautifully correct.

enchant (ehn CHANT)
To enchant is to put someone or something under a magic spell.

encipher (ehn SY fuhr)
To encipher is to take a secret message and write it in a code or a cipher.

Etruscan (ih TRUHS kuhn)
The Etruscans were an ancient people who lived in what is now northern Italy.

etymologist (eht uh MAHL uh jihst)
An etymologist is someone who studies the history of words.

exuberant (ehg ZOO buhr uhnt)
Anyone who is exuberant is very happy and overflowing with good feelings.

fanatic (fuh NAT ihk)
A fanatic is someone who gets very excited about his or her feelings or beliefs.

ferocious (fuh ROH shuhs)
Anyone or anything that is ferocious is savagely cruel and brutal.

fiend (feend)
A fiend is an evil spirit or a very wicked or cruel person.

gallows (GAL ohz)
A gallows is a wooden structure used for hanging criminals.

gesture (JEHS chuhr)
A gesture is a movement of the hands, arms, or body, used with or without words to express a feeling or an idea.

hideous (HIHD ee uhs)
Anyone or anything that is hideous is frightful, ugly, or horrible.

hieroglyphics (hy uhr uh GLIHF ihks)
Hieroglyphics are pictures or symbols that stand for words, ideas, or sounds. The ancient Egyptians and others wrote in hieroglyphics.

homonym (HAHM uh nihm)
A homonym is one of two or more words that sound alike, and may be spelled alike, but have different meanings.

impresario (ihm preh SAH ree oh)
An impresario is the manager or director of an orchestra or opera.

impudent (IHM pyuh duhnt)
An impudent person is someone who is bold and rude.

Indo-European (IHN doh yur uh PEE uhn)
Indo-European is the name given to an ancient language once spoken in Europe. It also means the group of related languages spoken in India, western Asia, and Europe.

inscription (ihn SKRIHP shuhn)
Words or letters written on stone, metal, or paper is an inscription.

jargon (JAHR guhn)
Jargon is the language used by people in a special group or profession.

jest (jehst)
To jest is to joke, or to make fun of something or someone.

jovial (JOH vee uhl)
A jovial person is one who is jolly and full of fun.

lexicographer (lehk suh KAHG ruh fuhr)
A lexicographer is a person who writes or puts together a dictionary.

lexicon (LEHK suh kuhn)
A lexicon is a dictionary.

linguist (LIHNG gwihst)
A linguist is someone who studies the history and structure of languages.

Megalosaurus (mehg uh loh SAWR uhs)
A Megalosaurus was a large flesh-eating dinosaur that lived in prehistoric times.

mortal (MAWR tuhl)
The word *mortal* means "sure to die." It also means a human being.

officious (uh FIHSH uhs)
An officious person minds others' business and offers unwanted advice.

ogle (OH guhl)
To ogle is to "make eyes" at or to look longingly at someone.

ornate (awr NAYT)
Anything that is ornate is highly decorated or showy.

palindrome (PAL ihn drohm)
A palindrome is a word or sentence that reads the same backward or forward.

pantaloons (pan tuh LOONZ)
Pantaloons are long, tight-fitting trousers worn in earlier times.

papyrus (puh PY ruhs)
Papyrus is a water plant from which ancient people made paper.

Phoenician (fuh NIHSH uhn)
The Phoenicians were an ancient seafaring people who lived at the eastern end of the Mediterranean Sea.

pompous (PAHM puhs)
A pompous person is someone who tries to seem important.

prim (prihm)
If you are prim, you are a very neat, proper, and formal person.

quake (kwayk)
To quake is to shake or tremble.

quash (kwahsh)
To quash is to crush or put down completely.

quill (kwihl)
A quill is a pen made from the hollow stem of a feather.

quintet (kwihn TEHT)
A quintet is a group of five—often five musicians.

rotund (roh TUHND)
Anything that is rotund is round and plump.

Semite (SEHM yt)
The Semites were people belonging to an ancient civilization in the Middle East.

sphinx (sfihngks)
In Greek myths, a sphinx is a monster with the head of a woman, the body of a lion, the tail of a snake, and the wings of a bird. Ancient Egyptian sphinxes had the head of a man and a lion's body. The most famous one, the Great Sphinx, is still standing.

Sumerian (soo MIHR ee uhn)
The Sumerians were an ancient people who lived in the Middle East.

symbol (SIHM buhl)
A symbol is something that stands for something else. The letters of the alphabet are symbols that stand for the sounds we make when we speak.

tedious (TEE dee uhs)
Anything that is tedious seems boring and tiresome.

tentacle (TEHN tuh kuhl)
A tentacle is one of the long, slender feelers on the head or around the mouth of an animal.

Thebes (theebz)
Thebes was the name of two ancient cities, one in Greece and one in Egypt.

therapist (THEHR uh pihst)
A therapist is a person trained to treat physical weaknesses or diseases in others. A speech therapist works with people who have difficulty speaking.

ubiquitous (yoo BIHK wuh tuhs)
Someone who is ubiquitous seems to be everywhere at once. Something that is ubiquitous seems to be present everywhere.

Viking (VY kihng)
The Vikings were seafaring warriors from Sweden, Norway, and Denmark. For several hundred years, they raided many parts of Europe.

vowel (VOW uhl)
A vowel is a speech sound formed by a stream of breath that is not stopped or changed by the tongue, teeth, or lips. The letters *a, e, i, o, u,* and sometimes *y,* are vowels.

xylophone (ZY luh fohn)
A xylophone is a musical instrument played by hitting flat wooden bars with small wooden hammers.

zany (ZAY nee)
To be zany is to act in a clownish, foolish way.

zealous (ZEHL uhs)
To be zealous is to be enthusiastic or eager.

zeppelin (ZEHP uh luhn or ZEHP luhn)
A zeppelin is a large, cigar-shaped balloon with a stiff frame. The engines and places for passengers or freight hang from the bottom.

Illustration Acknowledgments

The publishers of *Childcraft* gratefully acknowledge the courtesy of the following photographers, agencies, and organizations for illustrations in this volume. When all the illustrations for a sequence of pages are from a single source, the inclusive page numbers are given. In all other instances, the page numbers refer to facing pages, which are considered as a single unit or spread. All illustrations are the exclusive property of the publishers of *Childcraft* unless names are marked with an asterisk (*).

Cover: Françoise Nicolas Fried

1–9: Robert Byrd
10–15: Phillip Wende
16–23: Jerry Pinkney
24–25: Phillip Wende
26–27: Jerry Pinkney
28–41: Phillip Wende
42–45: Jerry Pinkney
46–47: Robert Byrd
48–65: Phillip Wende
66–67: Robert Byrd
68–73: Max Ranft
74–75: Paul Williams
76–81: Brian Froud
82–87: Max Ranft
88–91: Paul Williams
92–99: Ronald LeHew
100–101: Paul Williams
102–109: Kinuko Craft
110–111: Max Ranft
112–113: Robert Masheris
114–123: Kinuko Craft
124–125: Robert Masheris
126–127: Robert Byrd
128–139: John Magine
140–141: Robert Byrd
142–143: Jerry Pinkney
144–145: Oriental Institute, University of Chicago (*); *Childcraft* photos
146–147: Oriental Institute, University of Chicago (*); *Childcraft* photo; Metropolitan Museum of Art, New York, Gift of John D. Rockefeller, Jr., 1932 (*)
148–149: George G. Cameron, American Schools of Oriental Research and University of Michigan (*)
150–157: Brian Froud
158–159: *World Book* photo; Oriental Institute, University of Chicago (*)
160–161: Jerry Pinkney
162–163: Jerry Pinkney; British Museum (*)
164–165: Jerry Pinkney; *Childcraft* Art
166–167: Semitic Museum, Harvard University (*); Jerry Pinkney
168–169: Jerry Pinkney; Brown Brothers (*)
170–171: Jerry Pinkney
172–173: Jerry Pinkney; Kelsey Museum of Archaeology, University of Michigan (*); Museum of Fine Arts, Boston, Henry Lillie Pierce Residuary Fund and Bartlett Collection (*)
174–175: Jerry Pinkney
176–177: Bettmann Archive (*); Jerry Pinkney
180–181: Alinari (*); Pierpont Morgan Library
182–185: Jerry Pinkney
186–209: Braille, flag, and finger alphabets: Jack Wallen; art: Robert Byrd
212–213: Robert Byrd
214–229: *Childcraft* photos
230–231: Robert Byrd
232–233: Dave and Shirley Beckes
234–235: John Huehnergarth
236–237: Dick Martin
238–239: Dick Martin; Dave and Shirley Beckes
240–241: Dick Martin
242–243: Dave and Shirley Beckes
244–245: Robert Masheris
246–247: Sharon Elzuardia
248–249: Dave and Shirley Beckes; *Childcraft* art
250–251: Sharon Elzuardia; *Childcraft* art; Jack Wallen
252–253: Dave and Shirley Beckes
254–255: Dick Martin; Jack Wallen
256–257: Robert Masheris
258–259: Dick Martin
260–261: Sharon Elzuardia
262–263: John Huehnergarth
264–265: Dick Martin
266–267: John Huehnergarth
268–269: Sharon Elzuardia
270–271: *Childcraft* art; Dave and Shirley Beckes
272–273: Dick Martin
274–275: John Huehnergarth
276–277: Dick Martin
278–281: John Huehnergarth
282–285: Sharon Elzuardia
286–287: *Childcraft* art
288–289: Sharon Elzuardia

Index

This index is an alphabetical list of the important things covered in both words and pictures in this book. The index shows you what page or pages each thing is on. For example, if you want to find out what the book tells about a particular subject, such as the Greek alphabet, look under **Greek alphabet** or **alphabet.** You will find a group of words, called an entry, like this: **Greek alphabet,** 170-172, *with pictures.* This entry tells you that you can read about the Greek alphabet on pages 170-172. The words *with pictures* tell you that there are pictures of the Greek alphabet on these pages, too. Sometimes, the book only tells you about a thing and does not show a picture. Then, the words *with picture* will not be in the entry. It will look like this: **pig Latin** (secret language), 289. Sometimes, there is *only* a picture of a thing in the book. Then the word *picture* will appear before the page number, like this: **Arch of Titus** (Rome), *picture,* 180.

a (letter), *pictures,* 186
Aborigines, Australian (people)
　English words from, 113; 130
accent, *see* **dialect**
accent, foreign, 138-139
Africa, English words from, 113
alphabet, 182-185; *pictures,*
　186-209
　Braille, *pictures,* 186-209; 249,
　　with pictures
　finger, *pictures,* 186-209; 251
　flag, *pictures,* 186-209; 255,
　　with pictures; 282
　Gaelic, *picture,* 210-211
　Greek, 170-172, *with pictures;*
　　pictures, 178-179
　Hebrew, *picture,* 210-211
　lower-case letters, 180, *with
　　picture*
　Phoenician, 168-169, *with
　　pictures; pictures,* 178-179
　Roman, 174-176, *with pictures;
　　pictures,* 178-179
　Russian, *picture,* 210-211
　Semitic, 164-166, *with pictures;
　　pictures,* 178-179
alphabet cipher, 283
Angles (people), 72-73
Anglo-Saxon (language), *see*
　Old English
animal
　family names from, 64-65, *with
　　picture*
　origin of names, 16-19
Arabia, English words from, 112
Arch of Titus (Rome), *picture,* 180
Assyrian cuneiform (writing),
　picture, 147

astronaut, origin of word, 44
attic, origin of word, 22
Australia
　dialects, 137
　English language, 128-131,
　　with pictures
　slang, 130
automobile, origin of word, 44
**Aztec Indians, English words
　from,** 112

b (letter), *pictures,* 187
barber, origin of word, 30
beetle, origin of word, 17
Behistun Rock (Iran)
　cuneiform on, 148-149,
　　with pictures
Beowulf, story about, 76-80
book
　editor, 221
　origin of word, 28
　writing, 215-217, *with pictures*
box cipher, 286, *with picture*
Braille alphabet, *pictures,*
　186-209
　pun with, 249, *with pictures*
breakfast, origin of word, 24
Britannia (early name for
　England)
　Angles and Saxons, 72-73
　Roman rule, 70-71
British (people)
　dialects of, 136
　slang of, 130-131
bus, origin of word, 34-36, *with
　picture*

c (letter), *pictures,* 188
Caesar, Julius, cipher used by,
　283
Canada, dialects of, 137
Canterbury Tales, The, story
　from, 92-99
capital letter
　alphabet, *pictures,* 186-209
　Roman, 180, *with picture;
　　picture,* 176
careers, *see* **jobs**
catchup, origin of word, 13-14
Celts (people), 70-71
**Champollion, Jean François,
　study of hieroglyphics by,**
　162-163, *with picture*
Chaucer, Geoffrey (author)
　Chauntecleer and the Fox, 92-99
Chauntecleer and the Fox (story),
　92-99
Chinese (language), **English
　words from,** 112
Christmas Carol, A, story from,
　114-123
cipher, 288
　alphabet, 283
　box, 286, *with picture*
　number, 284-285
　pigpen, 287, *with picture*
clam chowder, origin of name, 10
clay tablet, writing on, 145-146,
　with pictures
clerk, origin of word, 30-31
clothes, origin of word, 27
cockney (people)
　dialect, 136
　slang, 130-131
code, 282

300

coleslaw, origin of word, 12-13
conundrum (riddle), 244-247
copywriter, work of, 225, *with pictures*
creative writer, work of, 215-217, *with pictures*
crocodile, origin of word, 16-17
crossword puzzle, 240-241, *with pictures*
cuneiform (writing), 143-146, *with pictures*
  story translated from, 150-157, *with pictures*
  study of, 148-149, *with pictures*
cursive script (writing), 180

d (letter), *pictures,* 189
deciphering, 288
  see also cipher
denims, origin of word, 27
dialect, 134-137, *with pictures*
  effect of newscasting on, 223
Dickens, Charles (author)
  Christmas Carol, A, 114-123
dictionary, 227-228
  spelling, 132-133
duck, origin of word, 17-18
dungarees, origin of word, 27
Dutch (language), English words from, 113

e (letter), *pictures,* 190-191
editor, work of, 221, *with pictures*
Egyptian hieroglyphics (writing), 158-159, *with pictures*
  study of, 160-163, *with pictures*
Elizabethan Age
  English language in, 100-101
  Midsummer Night's Dream, A (play), 102-108
  words from other languages, 110-113
engineer, origin of word, 32-33
England
  Angles and Saxons, 72-73
  dialects, 136-137
  English language, 128-131, *with pictures*
  Roman rule, 70-71
English language
  alphabet, 182-185; *pictures,* 186-209
  dialects, 134-137, *with pictures*
  foreign accents, 138-139

English language *(continued)*
  growth of, 110-113; 124-125
    Angles and Saxons, 72-73
    beginnings, 70-71; 88-89
    Elizabethan Age, 100-101; 102-108
    Middle English, 90; 92-99
    Modern English, 114-123
    Norman Conquest, 86-87
    Old English or Anglo-Saxon, 74-75; 76-80; 88-89
    Roman influence, 82-83
    Viking influence, 84-85
  in America, 128-131, *with pictures;* 133
  in Australia, 128-131, *with pictures*
  in Britain, 128-131, *with pictures;* 133
  study of, 227-229, *with pictures*
  word origins, 40-41
    animal names, 16-19
    cities in England, 71
    clothing, 26-27
    foods, 10-15
    invented words, 42-44
    job names, 30-33
    meals, 24-25
    noise-words, 38
    parts of house, 21-23
    school words, 28-29
    shortened words, 34-37
Eskimo (people), English words from, 113
etymologist, work of, 228-229

f (letter), *pictures,* 192
family name, *see* last name, origin of
fan, origin of word, 37
finger alphabet, *pictures,* 186-209
  palindrome with, 251, *with pictures*
first name, meaning of, 48-53, *with pictures*
fish, Sumerian writing of, 146, *with picture*
flag alphabet, *pictures,* 186-209; 282
  tongue twister, 255, *with pictures*
food, origin of names, 10-15
foreign accent, 138-139
French (language), English words from, 86-89
French fries, origin of name, 13

g (letter), *pictures,* 193
Gaelic alphabet, *picture,* 210-211
games with words, *see* word games
Gilgamesh, story about, 150-157, *with pictures*
given name, meaning of, 48-53, *with pictures*
Gold Bug, The (story), cipher from, 288
Gree (secret language), 289
Greek alphabet, 170-172, *with pictures; pictures,* 178-179
grocer, origin of word, 33
gun, origin of word, 36

h (letter), *pictures,* 193
hamburger, origin of word, 11
Hebrew alphabet, *picture,* 210-211
hieroglyphics (writing), 158-159, *with pictures*
  study of, 160-163, *with pictures*
hippopotamus, origin of word, 16
homonym, puns with, 248-249
house, parts of, 21-23

i (letter), *pictures,* 194; 184-185
ice-cream sundae, origin of name, 14-15
India, English words from, 112
Indian, American, English words from, 113
Indo-European (language), 229
International Flag Code, *pictures,* 186-209; 282
  tongue twister with, 255, *with pictures*
invention, words for, 42-44
invisible writing, 281
Italian (language), English words from, 112

j (letter), 184-185; *pictures,* 195
Japanese (language), English words from, 113
jargon, 223
jeans, origin of name, 26-27
jobs
  copywriter, 225, *with pictures*
  creative writer, 215-217, *with pictures*

jobs *(continued)*
editor, 221, *with pictures*
etymologist, 228-229
family names from, 58-59, *with pictures*
lexicographer, 227-228
linguist, 227-229, *with picture*
names, origin of, 30-33
newscaster, 223, *with pictures*
newspaper reporter, 219, *with pictures*
Journey of Gilgamesh (story), 150-157, *with pictures*
Julius Caesar, cipher used by, 283
Jutes (people), 72-73

k (letter), *pictures,* 196
ketchup, origin of word, 13-14
kitchen, origin of word, 22-23

l (letter), *pictures,* 197
language
beginnings, 68-69
dialects, 134-137, *with pictures*
foreign accents, 138-139
slang, 128-131, *with pictures*
spelling, 132-133
study of, 227-229, *with pictures*
Egyptian hieroglyphics, 160-163, *with pictures*
Sumerian cuneiform, 148-149, *with pictures*
writing, development of, 143-146, *with pictures*
see also **alphabet; English language; word games; word origins**
last name, origin of, 54-55, *with pictures*
from animals, 64-65, *with picture*
from father's name, 56-57, *with pictures*
from jobs, 58-59, *with pictures*
from nicknames, 60-61, *with picture*
from places, 62-63, *with picture*
Latin (language), **English words from,** 82-83
layout for advertisement, 225
letters of the alphabet, *see* **alphabet**
Levi's, origin of name, 27

lexicographer, work of, 227-228
linguist, work of, 227-229, *with picture*
lower-case letter, 180, *with picture*
alphabet, *pictures,* 186-209
lunch, origin of word, 24-25

m (letter), *pictures,* 198
magazine editor, work of, 221, *with pictures*
mail carrier, origin of name, 31-32
Malaya, English words from, 113
meal, origin of names, 24-25
Megalosaurus (prehistoric animal), **origin of name,** 19
Middle English (language), 90
Chauntecleer and the Fox (story), 92-99
Midsummer Night's Dream, A (play), 102-108
moose, origin of word, 18
Mr. Fister's Tongue Twister, 252-253, *with pictures*

n (letter), *pictures,* 198
Na (secret language), 289
name, origin of
animals, 16-19
cities in England, 71
clothing, 26-27
food, 10-15
invented words, 42-44
jobs, 30-33
meals, 24-25
parts of house, 21-23
school words, 28-29
shortened words, 34-37
see also **word origins**
name, personal
first, meaning of, 48-53, *with pictures*
last, origin of, 54-55, *with pictures*
from animals, 64-65, *with picture*
from father's name, 56-57, *with pictures*
from jobs, 58-59, *with pictures*
from nicknames, 60-61, *with picture*
from places, 62-63, *with picture*

naughty, changed meaning of, 41
Netherlands, English words from, 113
New England accent, 134-137
newscaster, work of, 223, *with pictures*
newspaper
editor, 221
reporter, 219, *with pictures*
New Zealand, dialects of, 137
nice, changed meaning of, 40
nickname, last names from, 60-61, 64-65, *with pictures*
noise-words, 38
Normans (people)
conquest of England, 86-87
words from, 88-89
number cipher, 284-285

o (letter), *pictures,* 199
octopus, origin of word, 18-19
Old English or **Anglo-Saxon** (language), 74-75
Beowulf, story about, 76-80
words from, 88-89
omnibus (vehicle), 34-36, *with picture*

p (letter), *pictures,* 199
palindrome (puzzle), 250-251, *with pictures*
pane, origin of word, 21-22
pants, origin of word, 26-27
paper
papyrus, 159
parchment, 180
papyrus, 159
parchment, 180
parent language, 229
pen, origin of word, 29
pencil, origin of word, 29
Persian (language), **English words from,** 112
personal name, *see* **name, personal**
Phoenician alphabet, 168-169, *with pictures; pictures,* 178-179
photograph, origin of word, 44
pictograph (writing), 143-146, *with pictures*
see also **cuneiform; hieroglyphics**
Picts (people), 71-73

picture language
  hieroglyphics, 158-163, *with pictures*
  rebus, 232-239, 240, *with pictures*
  Sumerian cuneiform, 143-157, *with pictures*
pig Latin (secret language), 289
pigpen cipher, 287, *with picture*
Poe, Edgar Allan (author), **cipher from story by,** 288
poodle, origin of word, 17
Portuguese (language), **English words from,** 112
prehistoric man, language of, 68-69
pronunciation, 134-137, *with pictures*
  effect of newscasting on, 223
pun, 248-249, *with pictures*
pupil, origin of word, 29
puzzle
  conundrum, 244-247
  crossword, 240-241, *with pictures*
  palindrome, 250-251, *with pictures*
  rebus, 232-239, *with pictures*
  riddle, 242-243, *with pictures*

q (letter), *pictures,* 200-201
quick, changed meaning of, 41

r (letter), *pictures,* 202
radio newscaster, 223
Rawlinson, Henry, study of cuneiform by, 148-149
rebus (puzzle), 232-239, *with pictures*
  crossword, 240, *with pictures*
reporter
  newscaster, 223, *with pictures*
  newspaper, 219, *with pictures*
research, 215; *pictures,* 216
riddle
  conundrum, 244-247
  Riddle of the Terrible Sphinx, 242-243, *with pictures*
Roman alphabet, 174-176, *with pictures; pictures,* 178-179
roof, origin of word, 23
Rosetta Stone (Egypt), **hieroglyphics on,** 163, *with picture*
Russian (language)
  alphabet, *picture,* 210-211
  English words from, 112

s (letter), *pictures,* 203
sandwich, origin of word, 11-12
Saxons (people), 72-73
school, origin of word, 28
secret languages, 289
secret messages, 280-288, *with pictures*
Semitic alphabet, 164-166, *with pictures; pictures,* 178-179
Shakespeare, William (author)
  Midsummer Night's Dream, A (play), 102-108
shingle, origin of word, 23
sign language, *pictures,* 186-209
  palindrome with, 251, *with pictures*
silly, changed meaning of, 41
slang (language), 128-131, *with pictures*
Southern accent, 134-137
Spanish (language), **English words from,** 112
speech therapist, work of, 229, *with picture*
spelling, 132-133
  game with, 268
Sphinx, Riddle of the, 242-243, *with pictures*
spider, origin of word, 17
storyboard for commercial, 225, *with picture*
Sumerian writing, *see* **cuneiform**
sundae, origin of word, 14-15
supper, origin of word, 25

t (letter), *pictures,* 203
teacher, work of, 229, *with pictures*
telephone, origin of word, 43
television
  commercial, 225, *with pictures*
  newscaster, 223, *with pictures*
  origin of word, 43-44
teller, origin of word, 31
Titus, Arch of (Rome), *picture,* 180
tongue twister, 186-209, 252-255, *with pictures*

u (letter), *pictures,* 204-205
United States
  dialects, 134-137, *with pictures*
  slang, 128-131, *with pictures*
  spelling, 132-133

v (letter), *pictures,* 206
Vikings (people), **English words from,** 84-85
villain, changed meaning of, 40-41

w (letter), *pictures,* 207
  origin of, 182-183
wall, origin of word, 23
Washington, George, code used by, 282
West Indies, English words from, 113
window, origin of word, 21
windowpane, origin of word, 21-22
word games
  Action Spelling Bee, 268
  Anagrams, 278-279
  A Was An Apple Pie, 262
  Birds, Beasts, Fishes, or Flowers, 267
  Calling All Cities, 258
  Categories, 275, *with picture*
  cipher, 283-285; 286-287, *with pictures*
  code, 282
  crossword puzzle, 240-241, *with pictures*
  Dumb Crambo, 264-265
  Fruit Basket Upset, 269
  Grocery Store, 260
  Hangman, 271
  I Love My Love, 264
  invisible writing, 281
  Minister's Cat, 265
  My Grandmother Likes Tea, 256, *with pictures*
  Our Cook Doesn't Like Peas, 257
  palindrome, 250-251, *with pictures*
  pun, 248-249, *with pictures*
  Puzzle Box, 270, *with picture*
  rebus, 232-239, *with pictures*
  riddle, 242-247, *with pictures*
  Scrambled Names, 272-273
  secret languages, 289
  Secret Word, 269, *with pictures*
  Snip, 267
  Spell-O, 276-277, *with picture*
  Squeeze, 274
  Teapot, 263
  tongue twister, 252-255, *with pictures*
  Where Are You Going?, 266
  Word Hunt, 261
  Word Snap, 259

word origins
astronaut, 44
attic, 22
automobile, 44
barber, 30
beetle, 17
book, 28
breakfast, 24
bus, 34-36, *with picture*
catchup, 13-14
clam chowder, 10
clerk, 30-31
coleslaw, 12-13
crocodile, 16-17
denims, 27
duck, 17-18
dungarees, 27
engineer, 32-33
fan, 37
French fries, 13
from other languages, 110-113
grocer, 33
gun, 36
hamburger, 11
hippopotamus, 16
ice-cream sundae, 14-15
jeans, 26-27
ketchup, 13-14
kitchen, 22-23
Levi's, 27
lunch, 24-25

word origins *(continued)*
mail carrier, 31-32
Megalosaurus, 19
moose, 18
naughty, 41
nice, 40
noise-words, 38
octopus, 18-19
pane, window, 21-22
pants, 26-27
pen, 29
pencil, 29
photograph, 44
poodle, 17
pupil, 29
quick, 41
roof, 23
sandwich, 11-12
school, 28
shingle, 23
silly, 41
spider, 17
supper, 25
telephone, 43
television, 43-44
teller, 31
villain, 40-41
wall, 23
window, 21
windowpane, 21-22
work, *see* **jobs**

writing (career)
copywriter, 225, *with pictures*
creative writer, 215-217, *with pictures*
editor, 221, *with pictures*
newscaster, 223, *with pictures*
newspaper reporter, 219, *with pictures*
writing (language)
ancient
cuneiform, 143-157, *with pictures*
hieroglyphics, 158-163, *with pictures*
ciphers, 283-285; 286-287, *with pictures*
codes, 282
invisible, 281
see also **alphabet**

x (letter), *pictures,* 207

y (letter), *pictures,* 208

z (letter), *pictures,* 209